The Gospel of Christian Freedom

The Gospel
of Christian Freedom

Quentin Quesnell

Herder and Herder

1969
HERDER AND HERDER NEW YORK
232 Madison Avenue, New York, N.Y. 10016

Foreword

BY JOHN L. MCKENZIE, S.J.

The reader of the New Testament, whether his reading is limited to liturgical passages or covers the entire collection, may be impressed by the amount of space which is given in the New Testament to Jewish-Christian controversy, and in particular to the controversy about the retaining of Jewish law and Jewish rites in the Church. To the reader this will seem to be a disproportionate amount of space for a problem which appears to him entirely irrelevant for the modern Church: and he may conclude that much of the New Testament is irrelevant for the modern Church. The Epistle of Paul to the Galatians, which deals entirely with the Jewish-Christian controversy, is surely an outstanding example of irrelevance. What does Paul's contrived allegory of the two wives of Abraham representing the slave Church and the free Church mean for us today—or what did it mean for the Galatians?

Yet I remember a serious student of the Bible who once said, after some years of work with the New Testament, "You know, Pharisaism is really the enemy." This student had achieved an understanding not easily reached, the understanding that the Jewish-Christian controversy touched on a basic and permanent issue, and that the New Testament Church, when it resolved this controversy, took its most decisive step towards the affirmation

v

of its identity. The issue, I said, is permanent, by which I mean that it has never been resolved in such a way that it cannot arise again; but the New Testament furnishes the principles by which the issue can be met.

It is difficult to give a name to this issue just because it returns in so many forms. Could it be more easily defined, it could be perhaps permanently resolved. As Paul met the issue, it was what seems to us the archaic question of whether Christians had to observe the Jewish law. We would be inclined to say that it makes no difference, that the Christian should be free to do it or not. But the question was not posed in terms of freedom, and this is precisely where the basic issue is discerned. It was a question of freedom, and Paul met the question by affirming Christian freedom. It was a question whether Christ had really saved us, or whether his saving act had to be supplemented by something else. If Christ has really saved us, then we are free of obligations to the law. The Christian has only one obligation laid upon him by Jesus, the obligation to love his neighbor as himself. No one can add to this obligation or improve upon the style of life which this obligation creates.

But the free Church has never detached herself from the slave Church; and Pharisaism remains the enemy. Pharisaism here means the attitude which believes that there has to be a "law," if not the law of Moses then some other law, that Christian freedom is not enough to assure that the saving act of Jesus be effective. Law then becomes suddenly primary, the real means by which one is saved. The love of one's neighbor as oneself can never be codified; it is achieved by an unending series of highly personal decisions which offer abundant occasions for error, even in good faith. But only the individual Christian can surely recognize the opportunities and the dangers which he encounters in his own experience. It seems easier and surer to accumulate a set of precise and well-defined obligations which one can understand and calculate. Law gives security in the knowledge that one has done all that one ought, or rather that one has done nothing which one ought not do. When this happens, the law of Moses has been re-enacted. The law replaces Christian freedom and Christian responsibility. Historic Catholicism has much more frequently appeared as a community of law than as a community of love.

There is surely no less urgency to proclaim and defend Christian freedom in the contemporary Church than there was in the Church of the apostles. But what modern churchman would write a pastoral letter the length of the Epistle to the Galatians with only one point, the point that Christ has freed the faithful from all obligations to the Law? To my knowledge no churchman has, and I do not know how he would find the language if he wished to write such a letter. For our church-talk does not deal with Christian freedom; we are much more facile when we speak of law, which may suggest that we have learned more from the Pharisees than we have from Paul. The question is more urgent for us than it was for Paul and the Galatians.

It is therefore a pleasure to introduce Quentin Quesnell's effort to paraphrase and interpret the Epistle to the Galatians for modern Catholics. The Epistle is really too radical for the twentieth-century church, and Quesnell has made its radicalism transparent. The reader may learn how far we have moved from Paul and in what direction; he will recognize, I hope, that we have moved towards Pharisaism. Jesus is quoted as saying of the Pharisees that they laid intolerably heavy burdens on men without lifting a finger to ease them. Paul knew that law regularly makes it difficult to love one's neighbor, and often makes it impossible. Quesnell leaves no doubt that Christianity and Pharisaism are irreconcilable.

The paraphrase often imitates Paul's breathless conversational style. It is hard to do this, but something of the spirit of Paul is captured. We modern theologians affect the detached and objective style of the professional scholar. This has some value, but it is not the way Paul talked. He spoke from genuine conviction and deep feelings; he was not talking about ideas but about persons, and he loved persons as Jesus has taught us to love them. He even loved the Pharisees, and rendered them the supreme service of preventing them from doing the harm of which they were capable. Most Bible readers find Paul an acquired taste, and some such revelation of his personal qualities as is attempted here may introduce them to an experience which is delightful once the taste is cultivated.

Will Quesnell reach the Pharisees? Probably not, even though, like Paul, he loves them; but it is of the essence of Pharisaism not to listen. Should he attract their attention, they may stone him or let him off with forty stripes save one; I speak metaphorically, of course. For Paul these occupational risks were real, not metaphorical. It seems that the proclamation of Christian freedom is more likely to arouse hostility than any other element of the Gospel. The greater the risk of hostility, the more manifest is the urgent need of the proclamation. I think that Paul would be shocked to see the power which the slave Church holds over the free Church. I thank Quentin Quesnell for speaking for the free Church.

Introduction

Christian faith and tradition have always insisted that the Bible somehow contains a message for believers of every time and place. The mechanics and metaphysics of this notion boggle the mind. Perhaps it could be rationalized in the following fashion: insofar as we, in faith, identify our faith-conviction with Paul's, we can hear in his explanation and preaching the echo of our own aspirations.

Still, why should we identify our faith with Paul's? There is no compelling reason to adopt this course. When we identify in this way, we do so by the same free choice by which we make any act of faith. Whatever lies behind our statement "I am a Christian" lies also behind our statement "I take Paul's view as an explanation of what 'being a Christian' is. I also believe that view is inspired. It then becomes 'object of faith' and 'word of God' to me."

Yet even this explanation is not enough. For Paul is neither addressing me directly nor speaking in the terms or context which I can directly understand. Interpretation is needed. At best I could only guess what Paul would say to me in my circumstances—if Paul, by his own careful interpretation, could ever fully understand me and my circumstances.

I certainly cannot say that the man who shares Paul's

1

understanding of the essence of Christianity would, in my circumstances today, say the same things Paul once said to the Galatians. Some of the things he said to them we cannot even understand today! Would he tell us things we cannot understand? Other warnings and exhortations he gives them are related to persons, things and phenomena which are now past. Would he then discuss them with us?

The relations between things and people inevitably change as society changes. Human institutions have a different meaning in the twentieth century. It is not very likely, for instance, that today Paul would urge slaves if indeed he could find any to obey their masters and not seek freedom (Ephesians 6, 5).

How do we go about reading something from another age as the word of God for contemporary Christians? As a start, we might try to grasp Paul's central thought or the reasons why he bothered to write to these people in the first place.

Which way shall our discussion go? It will necessarily move, I should think, in the direction in which we feel situations and circumstances have changed since Paul's time. It may be that the central religious problem for Paul is still a problem for us. It may be that today as then, good people are falling or are tempted to fall into certain basically false positions regarding religion and religiosity, regarding freedom, responsibility, and law. If this is so, then his letter, even as it stands, may open our eyes today to certain perennial realities concerning the God-man relationship. On the other hand, it may turn out that circumstances have so changed between his time and ours that it will require considerable effort to draw from his words anything of value for understanding our own situation. At any rate, it seems worth investigating, whatever the results. At the very least, we should gain in self-knowledge as we arrive at a somewhat better understanding of our origins.

It would be foolish to deny, of course, that the letter to the Galatians is less than the whole picture of New Testament theology. It is only one small part of the New Testament. It was written in response to a very special situation. It is not even a complete statement of the theology of St. Paul. Consequently, a book on Galatians suffers from all the limitations of the letter itself. It would be unreasonable to ask a book like this one to fill in the entire picture of New Testament thought, completely rounded out to allow room, for instance, for such stark expressions of a different doctrine from Paul's as appear in Revelations 2, 14, 20.

This book can aim only at uncovering the meaning of this one document as Paul wrote it and the Galatians read it. It does so under the supposition, traditional enough in Christian theology, that there must have been some reason why this letter was, under God's providence, selected to be a part of the canon of sacred scripture; and under the further supposition, quite reasonable on the face of it, that whatever reason those early Christian generations had for admitting this letter into their list of sacred books, their decision was not unconnected with some perennial value they thought they saw in it. We seek to discover that value—with whatever interest it might carry for today.

It is quite probable that some points directly related to the reflections and concerns of the present-day church will be found in Galatians. Now as then the church is in a state of transition. The question of loyalty

3

to past traditions vs. adaption to present needs confronts us on every side, as it did Paul and his communities. The balance between authority and personal responsibility, personal response to inspiration, and the roles of love and of obedience are very much with us.

Many modern Catholics feel they were taught in their youth an approach to God quite different from that which the church seems to be urging on them at the present hour. Many Catholics used to emphasize exactness in form and ritual in a manner discouraged by the liturgical reforms following Vatican II. Many Catholics were raised with the impression that a "good" Catholic was one who attempted to observe all God's laws—both those divinely revealed and those later formulated by the church. Even Catholics who felt called to do something more, to go all the way in giving themselves to God's service and love, often found the church pointed them towards religious communities, where further laws were added. They found that the ideal of Christian perfection proposed to them was the perfect fulfillment of all these laws and rules, perfect obedience and submission to the rules left by the founder of their congregation, as well as to all the additional rules, regulations, and decisions which their religious superiors had made or would make for them. This emphasis on law has come in for a certain amount of questioning in recent times.

Abundant parallels to these issues can be found in the background of the Epistle to the Galatians. The religious tradition in which Paul and his fellow Christians had been brought up was the tradition of the Old Testament, of the Jewish Law. The good Jew loved God and expressed that love by exact fulfillment of everything God had commanded. This same law of God, given at length in the pages of the Old Testament, cherished and even expanded by faithful tradition, had continued normative for the first apostles and for the first Christian community, which was in the city of Jerusalem—the capital of Judaism. The Christians of those first ten or twenty years were apparently identifiable only as a sect within Judaism. They were the Jews who believed that Jesus of Nazareth was the promised Messiah. Paul knew of that sect and says he persecuted its members (1, 13) and tried to destroy their community. He connects this activity with his "extreme zeal for the traditions of my fathers" (1, 14).

But when Paul himself was converted to Christianity he had a revelation of what Christianity could be. He saw something in the fact of recognizing Jesus as the promised Messiah which implied for him liberation from the Law. He saw that believing in this crucified man as God's promised Messiah implied that a new norm of right conduct and human goodness had been given to men. The Law became irrelevant; or rather, only one law now applied—the law of a love like Christ's. When Paul began preaching Christianity to those who had not been born and raised as Jews he preached only this: faith in Christ crucified and a morality based on a deep appreciation for what faith in a crucified Lord implies.

Paul did give his Gentile converts instruction in the Old Testament. This is clear from the way he argues from and about the Old Testament in this letter. To someone unfamiliar with the Old Testament this letter would have been obscure indeed. But while teaching them the history of God's love and care for Israel as witnessed by the Old Testament, Paul did *not* tell the Gentiles that they had to observe the laws with which so much of the Old Testament occupied itself.

But with that, the seeds of discord and trouble were

5

sown. Paul received pagans into Christian faith and set up supposedly Christian communities without imposing the obligations of the Law. What a shock and scandal that must have been to those who were Christians before them—all devout Jews, who had come to know God from the Old Testament, and had lived lives of love and service to God through observance of his Law.

"What could this mean?" they must have asked. "Men calling themselves religious, turning to God in Christ, without accepting God's clear commands to men given in the Law?" Protests were probably made directly to Paul. Discontent was certainly conveyed to the Gentile members of Paul's communities. The latter were given the impression Paul had robbed them of something. And in their own zeal for the fullest and most generous service of God, the Galatians apparently listened to the objections, took them seriously, and began to practice the Mosaic Law.

Paul writes this letter to rebuke the Galatians strongly for taking up this spirituality based on law and obedience to law. He touches on the question of observing the feasts and fasts commanded by the Law: "You observe days and months and seasons and years! I am afraid I have labored over you in vain" (4, 10f.).

He comments on the Law's strict circumcision requirement: "If you receive circumcision, Christ will be of no advantage to you. . . . You are severed from Christ, you who would be justified by the Law. You have fallen away from grace" (5, 2–4).

He writes about observing the Jewish laws of purity in regard to certain foods: "But when Cephas came to Antioch I opposed him to his face, because he stood condemned. For before certain men came from James, he ate with the Gentiles; but when they came he drew back and separated himself, fearing the circumcision party. And with him the rest of the Jews acted insincerely, so that even Barnabas was carried away by their insincerity. But when I saw that they were not straightforward about the truth of the gospel, I said to Cephas before them all: 'If you, though a Jew, live like a Gentile and not like a Jew, how can you compel the Gentiles to live like Jews?' " (2, 11–14).

Of all the demands of the Law, he speaks most about the requirements of circumcision. There are "those who would compel you to be circumcised" (6, 12). But he insists that "in Christ Jesus neither circumcision nor uncircumcision is of any avail" (5, 6) ; "Neither circumcision counts for anything nor uncircumcision" (6, 15). He warns them, "Stand fast therefore, and do not submit again to a yoke of slavery" (5, 1). "If you receive circumcision, Christ will be of no advantage to you" (5, 2). "I testify to every man who receives circumcision, that he is bound to keep the whole Law" (5, 3).

The letter is full of indications that Paul is too late. Many in the Galatian community have already made their choice in favor of observing the Law: "Tell me, you who desire to be under the Law . . ." (4, 21). "You are severed from Christ, you who would be justified by the Law; you have fallen away from grace" (5, 4). "You were running well; who hindered you from obeying the truth? This persuasion is not from him who called you. A little yeast leavens the whole lump" (5, 7–3). "Oh foolish Galatians, who has bewitched you?" (3, 1). "I am astonished that you are so quickly deserting him who called you in the grace of Christ and turning to a different gospel . . ." (1, 6).

7

The fault is with certain teachers and preachers working in the Galatian community: "There are some who trouble you and want to pervert the gospel of Christ" (1, 7). "He who is troubling you will bear his judgment, whoever he is" (5, 10). "I wish those who unsettle you would mutilate themselves" (5, 12). Their motives are not fully clear to us; but it is obvious that Paul esteems them none too highly. "It is those who want to make a good showing in the flesh that would compel you to be circumcised, and only in order that they may not be persecuted for the cross of Christ" (6, 12). "For even those who receive circumcision do not themselves keep the Law, but they desire to have you circumcised in order that they may glory in your flesh" (6, 13). "They make much of you, but to no good purpose, they want to shut you out, that you may make much of them" (4, 17). "Who hindered you from obeying the truth? This persuasion is not from him who called you" (5, 7f.). ". . . even if we or an angel from heaven should preach to you a gospel contrary to that which we preached to you, let him be accursed" (1, 7f.). "False brethren secretly brought in, who slipped in to spy out our freedom which we have in Christ Jesus, that they might bring us into bondage . . ." (2, 4).

The Gospel of Christian Freedom
Written by Paul to the People of Galatia

Text and Paraphrase

1, 1   This letter comes from PAUL. You know who I am,
or at least who I claim to be. I call myself AN
APOSTLE, a man sent from God. I have NOT been
sent FROM MEN. I know that in the mouths of my
enemies this is an accusation against me, that I
have no human authorization. But I admit it
gladly. I glory in it. I proclaim it loudly as a
fundamental point in what I preach: My call came
NOT THROUGH MAN. BUT it came only THROUGH
JESUS CHRIST AND GOD THE FATHER WHO RAISED HIM
FROM THE DEAD.

This means I begin writing to you with a call
to faith. But that should not surprise you. You
must remember that my original coming was no
different. You heard me then in faith—and so I
ask you to hear me now—or refuse to hear me at
all. My message is difficult, incredible, fantastic.
It is a scandal to human ears. I claim it comes
from God, and if it does, it is to be believed, no
matter how scandalous it sounds. But if you doubt
that it truly comes from God, then look elsewhere,
for I do not pretend to be able to convince you of
the truth of my message by appealing to other
authorities. What could they possibly add? What
"informed sources" or "ancient traditions" or

11

"legitimate superiors" could add one milligram of truth to a message of salvation or subtract one iota from it? They cannot make salvation come true; they cannot give it themselves; and therefore they cannot promise it either—except in God's name. Well, it is in his name that I am claiming to speak. The fact that five or fifty or five hundred thousand others stood at my side would not really change the situation, would it? The question is not who or how many preach this doctrine. The question is: is the doctrine from God? And no number of human witnesses can ever make that more or less believable, can they? I speak in the name of God because I am conscious that what I say is God's own word for the salvation of the world. If you recognize what I say for being just that, you will believe it; if you do not, you will reject it. And the number of sources or authorities to which I appealed would not make any difference anyway.

1, 2 AND this letter comes from ALL THE BROTHERS who are WITH ME too, and it is directed TO THE CHURCHES OF GALATIA.

1, 3 GOD'S GIFT BE YOURS AND PEACE BE YOURS FROM GOD OUR FATHER AND FROM THE LORD JESUS CHRIST.

This is my wish for you as it is God's wish for you. And mentioning it leads me to the heart of the message I have preached to you once before as God's message of salvation:

1, 4 HE (Jesus Christ, Lord) GAVE HIMSELF FOR OUR SINS IN ORDER TO RESCUE US FROM OUT OF THE WICK-EDNESS OF THE WORLD WE LIVE IN.

This is, you remember, the faith I preached. Jesus was a man chosen by God—we call him Christ,

12

"the anointed one." He was chosen by God for a special mission and he freely accepted and fulfilled that mission. The mission was to bear God's message and to *be* God's message to the world—to us. For us to try to express that message in words always results in what is only a pale imitation of the expression he gave that message when he died on the cross that he might be raised from the dead that we might believe. The message was that God loved men, cared about them, pursued and surrounded them with his love. The message was that God saved men from life's most appalling evils. God transformed evil into good. He brought men back from the dead. Giving himself to bear the message as he did, Jesus was giving himself for us. He was giving himself for us because we needed him, and we needed him because we needed his message. He thus became the victim of our necessities, made himself freely the victim of our necessities, and thus brought the message itself to perfection. For God's transformation of evil into good and God's salvation of suffering, dying men is achieved precisely by and through the free acts of free men, who choose to give themselves wholly for their fellow men and to their fellow men. So the message is not only, "God loves us," but also, "Let us love one another as he has loved us."

Christ gave himself to bear this message and to be this message because we needed it. Like all men, we needed it because we had pursued the paths of selfishness, hatred, cruelty, and fear; because we had fled one another and exploited one another and were now afraid and unable to give ourselves to one another. We needed divine assurance that the way of loving self-sacrifice is the way of life; that it is the one true hope of the world. We had lost that vision and lost that life. We were sinners. And Christ gave himself to be the saving message we needed because we were sinners. His was the only message which could save us out of the way of sin and death and turn us to God's way of love and life.

After him, all men might read and believe this message. And believing, they would find that it was true. Believing they would find that they had indeed escaped the limitations which sin had put on the time and place, the world in which they lived. Believing God's word as given in the crucified and risen Christ, men would find that the evils of the age and the world in which they had been born could neither bring them down nor even seriously hold them back. They would finally find themselves free to be what in their heart of hearts they had always wanted to be anyway. They would find they could not really fail, and certainly could never despair. They would know the world was good and that God was working out their further and perfect good in everything that happened to them.

This message—a thousand times more effectively and powerfully conveyed—was what God sent men in Christ. This is the message with which he wanted men ever after to be ultimately and decisively confronted. Christ died and rose as God's own Word. And this is the word I once brought you and recall to you now.

And he accomplished all ACCORDING TO THE WILL OF GOD AND OF OUR FATHER—TO HIM BE GLORY FOR EVER AND EVER. AMEN.

1, 5

14

When men believed this, then God would be truly glorified. For "That glory consists in this; that men knowingly, freely, and gratefully accept what God has achieved perfectly through Christ, and manifest it in their whole lives" (*Decree on the ministry and life of priests*, paragraph 2).

1, 6   I AM SURPRISED THAT YOU SO SOON FIND YOURSELVES MOVED AWAY FROM THE ONE WHO CALLED YOU IN A FREE GIFT OF CHRIST, AND ARE NOW TURNED TOWARD ANOTHER GOSPEL, another "message of good news."

1, 7   BUT IT IS NOT ANOTHER ONE—because there is no other. IT IS ONLY THAT SOME PEOPLE ARE RILING YOU UP AND ARE DOING THEIR BEST TO PERVERT THE

1, 8   ONE GOOD NEWS OF THE MESSIAH. BUT EVEN IF WE OURSELVES, brothers, even we who first brought you this news; if we OR, even if AN ANGEL FROM HEAVEN START PREACHING A MESSAGE THAT IS NOT THE MESSAGE WE HAVE PREACHED TO YOU, LET HIM GO TO HELL.

The right emphasis, brothers, is on the message itself, not the preacher. Your faith was in what I said, not in who I was or am. When I insist on my own independence, as I did at the beginning, it is not to build myself up above others or to make you dependent on me. It is to insist that you stop looking to the question of *who* says this or that, and concentrate instead on what is said.

Look at this message of mine. You have accepted it in faith. That means that you have believed it truly is God's message, not mine. If that is what you truly accept, if you really recognize God speaking in that message, then you can only cling to it unshakeably. Don't anyone take it away from you

—no matter what his credentials. If it is God's message, not Paul's message, then even if Paul himself should come again and try to take it away from you, you would resist. Even an angel could not dissuade you from it now. For you recognize the message as the very word of God—or, if you don't, you have not yet truly believed. For this recognition is our very faith.

1, 9   All right, brothers WE HAVE SAID THIS TO YOU BEFORE. I NOW SAY IT AGAIN IN JUST THE SAME WAY —IF ANYONE, ANYONE AT ALL, PREACHES A GOSPEL APART FROM THE ONE YOU HAVE ONCE RECEIVED in
1, 10 faith, TO HELL WITH HIM. AFTER ALL, what am I working at? AM I TRYING TO PERSUADE MEN about God's word? OR do you think I'm trying to sell some human word to GOD?

If it's God's word I am bringing to men, if it's men I am trying to convince, then I appeal to God as my authority, the only authority I can appeal to. Human tradition, human authority, human dignity and excellence can add nothing to that appeal. How could it? What can you add to God? Or, on the other hand, how many human supporters would I have had to line up in order to convince you that my message truly came from God? How many human testimonies suffice to demonstrate divine origin? How many human authorities must be added together to prove that behind a certain statement stands the authority of God?

Perhaps it would be different if I were trying to convince God of something human. Then the more human sources and authorities I could line up for my cause, the more impressive my argument would be. But that's not the case. I'm trying to convince men, as you well know. And so all I can do is give the message God gave me and challenge men to recognize it for what it is.

You do not think that ALL THIS EFFORT OF MINE IS DEVOTED TO PLEASING MEN, do you? IF I WERE TRYING TO PLEASE MEN, I WOULD NOT EVEN BE A SERVANT OF CHRIST. There is little to please men in the preaching of Christ crucified.

1, 11   NO, BROTHERS, ALLOW ME TO INFORM YOU: THE GOSPEL PREACHED BY ME IS NOT a message of good news PUT TOGETHER ACCORDING TO HUMAN FORMULAS.

1, 12   AND I DID NOT RECEIVE IT FROM ANY HUMAN BEING. I WAS NOT TAUGHT THIS GOSPEL BY ANY TEACHER. I GOT IT

1, 13   FROM A REVELATION OF JESUS MESSIAH. FOR YOU HAVE HEARD ABOUT MY WAY OF LIVING EARLIER when I was INSIDE OF JUDAISM. YOU KNOW THAT I WAS AN OUTSTANDING PERSECUTOR of the Christian community. AND I TRIED TO DESTROY THE ASSEMBLY OF GOD.

1, 14   AND IN MY PRACTICE OF JUDAISM, I RAN FAR BEYOND MY CONTEMPORARIES, PEOPLE OF MY OWN age and GENERATION. I WAS MOST OUTSTANDINGLY ZEALOUS FOR THE DEAR TRADITIONS RECEIVED FROM OUR FATHERS.

Commentary

Here Paul reveals what the so-called "other gospel" was that the people of Galatia were turning to. Here we see what "some people were riling them up about," "perverting the one good news of the Messiah." He had not explained himself so far because he did not have to. The people to whom he was writing were perfectly aware of what points their new preachers had made that contradicted Paul's earlier preaching.

Even here Paul does not stop to explain the exact point of the dispute. But he alludes to it unmistakably in the way he now begins to show his own background relative to the matter under dispute, that is, the question of "Judaism." It was an issue which terribly vexed the early church. This is not the infamous modern "Jewish question" raised by Hitler and people like him who look for a scapegoat for society's ills. It is rather the simple question of the binding force of the old-time Jewish Law. It is a problem which, at first sight, is not in any sense a problem for us today. No Christian normally worries that he does not observe the Sabbath—Saturday—as the Lord's day, abstaining from all manner of work on that day. No one thinks twice about violating the food laws—regulations which forbid the eating of pork, shrimp, oysters, and many other delicacies much appreciated by Christian palates today.

We have been raised to think of these things—if we have ever heard of them at all—as falling under "the Old Law." We have been taught that they were once forbidden to the Jewish people according to the laws of the Old Testament, but that the coming of Christ had changed all that. Since most of us never studied the Old Testament laws very seriously anyway, we do not stop to ask ourselves why Christ's coming should have changed it, or how or when this change was brought about. We do not stop to notice that if Christ's coming did change God's law for his people, still for some strange reason the earliest Christians knew nothing about this change for many years. And we do not reflect what a serious thing it would have been in those days to try to make and propagate such a change.

We read, for instance, the story in Mark 7, 1–23, in large part announcing this liberation from the Jewish Law. (Before rushing to conclude that this is a factual episode from the life of Jesus, it would be well to notice that Luke's gospel omits it and leaves the first revelation of the doctrine contained in it to the tenth chapter of the Acts of the Apostles—some time after the Ascension.) In Mark 7, 15ff., Jesus says, " 'There is nothing from outside a man that can go into him and make him unclean. . . . Do you not realize that everything from outside that goes into a man cannot make him unclean, because it does not go into his heart but into his belly and out it goes into the privy?' Thus he declared all foods clean." Here Jesus speaks in sharp, unmistakable terms of the foolishness of thinking that certain foods can defile a man in any spiritual sense. They go to his belly and out of his body; they cannot touch the heart. It is a very clear and very reasonable argument. We tend to sympathize with it because we were not ourselves raised to observe the food laws ridiculed here.

But to make more meaningful to us what the reaction of a Jew in Jesus' generation would have been to this criticism, we have to realize the attack really misses the point. The Jews did not think the foods rendered them unclean because they went into their hearts. The Jews knew that food passed through the human belly and drainage system. If they abstained from certain foods as unclean, it was because God's law had commanded them to do so. Leviticus 11, 41–45, for instance, says, "Every creeping thing that creeps upon the earth is an abomination to you. It shall not be eaten, . . . and you shall not render your souls abominable in all creeping things that creep upon the earth, and you shall not defile yourselves with them, and you shall not make yourselves unclean in them; because I am the Lord your God, and you shall be sanctified and you shall be holy, because I am holy, and you shall not defile your souls in all the creeping things that move upon the earth . . ."

The simple command of the law makes the food unclean for all those who want to live in faithful observance of God's law. To tell such people that the foods of themselves cannot defile their hearts is to miss the point: disobedience to God's law is the real defilement they are afraid of.

The unfairness of the argument may impress us more if it is turned against ourselves. Suppose an unbeliever stood by and laughed at our ceremony of baptism. "Do you not know that pouring water on the body cannot cleanse the soul? Water flows over the skin and back into the basin. Purity of heart must come from within a man's own heart and intention." The objection supposes that we Christians believe the water washes the soul. But of course we believe no such thing. Then why do we pour water in order to cleanse the soul in baptism? Because Christians believe this is God's sacrament, and that it must be performed in the way God wants. Rationalistic objections cannot affect the issue one way or the other.

Now the Jews of Jesus' and Paul's day believed they had received the law of God through Moses. This Law, written and unwritten, was handed down to them in "the traditions of the fathers." Observing the Law as perfectly as possible was the greatest sign of their love for God. It was the way of preserving God's favor for their

people. It was a continued sign in their midst that God
had chosen them out of all nations to be his special
people.

"Now this is the commandment, the statutes and the
ordinances which the Lord your God commanded me to
teach you, that you may do them in the land to which
you are going over, to possess it; that you may fear the
Lord your God, you and your son and your son's son, by
keeping all his statutes and his commandments, which
I command you, all the days of your life; and that your
days may be prolonged. Hear therefore, O Israel, and be
careful to do them; that it may go well with you, and
that you may multiply greatly, as the Lord, the God of
your fathers, has promised you, in a land flowing with
milk and honey" (Deuteronomy 6, 1–4).

"And now, Israel, what does the Lord your God require
of you, but to fear the Lord your God, to walk in all his
ways, to love him, to serve the Lord your God with all
your heart and with all your soul, and to keep the commandments and statutes of the Lord, which I command
you this day for your good?" (Deuteronomy 10, 12f.).

"And if you obey the voice of the Lord your God, being
careful to do all his commandments which I command
you this day, the Lord your God will set you high above
all the nations of the earth. And all these blessings shall
come upon you and overtake you, if you obey the voice of
the Lord your God. Blessed shall you be in the city, and
blessed shall you be in the field. Blessed shall be the fruit
of your body and the fruit of your ground, and the fruit of
your beasts . . ." (Deuteronomy 28, 1ff.).

"But if you will not obey the voice of the Lord your
God or be careful to do all his commandments and his
statutes which I command you this day, then all these

21

curses shall come upon you and overtake you. Cursed shall you be in the city, . . ." etc. (Deuteronomy, 28, 15ff.).

The history of the people of Israel as recounted in the books of Joshua, Judges, Samuel, and Kings was a checkered one regarding this observance of God's laws. As the authors of those books look back over the centuries which stretched from the time of Moses to their own day (from about the thirteenth to the sixth century B.C.) they saw a recurrent pattern of sin, punishment, forgiveness, followed by new sin, new divine punishment, new forgiveness, until finally the whole process climaxed in the ultimate punishment God's prophets had long been threatening—the nation was definitively conquered by its enemies, the holy city of Jerusalem was destroyed, and the people led away into exile in Babylon.

During the exile the people and their prophets reflected on their past. They resolved that the future would be different. They would keep the law of God if God ever allowed them to return to their own homes in Israel. They would keep it perfectly and forever. And so the prophet Ezekiel wrote for them, "Behold, I will take the people of Israel from the nations among which they have gone, and will gather them from all sides, and bring them to their own land; and I will make them one nation in the land, upon the mountains of Israel; and one king shall be king over them all . . . and they shall be my people and I will be their God. My servant David shall be king over them; and they shall all have one shepherd. They shall follow my ordinances and be careful to observe my statutes" (37, 21–24). Ezekiel also wrote, "The Levitical priests, the sons of Zadok, who kept the charge of my sanctuary when the people of Israel went astray from me, shall come near to me to minister to me . . . They shall teach my people the difference between the holy and the common, between the unclean and the clean. In a controversy they shall act as judges, and they shall judge it according to my judgments. They shall keep my laws and my statutes in all my appointed feasts, and they shall keep my sabbaths holy" (44, 15. 23f.).

The sincerity and the vigor with which the Jews set themselves to this task of following the law is portrayed for us in the books of Ezra and Nehemiah. A short summary of their view of life— of their own past history and future destiny and the role which obedience to the law must play in it—is given in the prayer of Ezra: "Thou art the Lord, thou alone; thou hast made heaven, the heaven of heavens, with all their host, the earth and all that is on it, the seas and all that is in them; and thou preservest all of them; and the host of heaven worships thee. Thou art the Lord, the God who didst choose Abram and bring him forth out of Ur of the Chaldeans and give him the name Abraham . . ." (Nehemiah 9, 6ff). The prayer goes on to praise God for making a promise to Abraham and fulfilling it; for liberating the people from their bondage in Egypt. Then it adds, "Thou didst come down upon Mount Sinai, and speak with them from heaven and give them right ordinances and true laws, good statutes and commandments, and thou didst make known to them thy holy sabbath and command them commandments and statutes and a law by Moses thy servant" (Nehemiah 9, 13f.).

"But they and our fathers acted presumptuously and stiffened their neck and did not obey thy commandments" (Nehemiah 9, 16). Then God's forgiveness is portrayed, and the way he finally brought them into the land he had promised them and subdued it beneath them and gave them prosperity.

"Nevertheless they were disobedient and rebelled against thee and cast thy law behind their back and killed thy prophets, who had warned them in order to turn them back to thee, and they committed great blasphemies. Therefore thou didst give them into the hand of their enemies, who made them suffer; and in the time of their suffering they cried to thee and thou didst hear them from heaven; and according to thy great mercies thou didst give them saviors who saved them from the hand of their enemies. But after they had rest they did evil again before thee, and thou didst abandon them to the hand of their enemies, so that they had dominion over them; yet when they turned and cried to thee thou didst hear from heaven and many times thou didst deliver them according to thy mercies. And thou didst warn them in order to turn them back to thy law. Yet they acted presumptuously and did not obey thy commandments, but sinned against thy ordinances, by the observance of which a man shall live, and turned a stubborn shoulder and stiffened their neck and would not obey. Many years thou didst bear with them, and didst warn them by thy Spirit through thy prophets; yet they would not give ear. Therefore thou didst give them into the hand of the people of the lands. Nevertheless in thy great mercies thou didst not make an end of them or forsake them; for thou art a gracious and merciful God" (Nehemiah 9, 26–31).

And so Ezra and the people resolve to make a covenant

with God once more "to walk in God's law which was given by Moses the servant of God, and to observe and do all the commandments of the Lord our God and his ordinances and his statutes. We will not give our daughters to the peoples of the land or take their daughters for our sons; and if the peoples of the land bring in wares or any grain on the sabbath day to sell, we will not buy from them on the sabbath or on a holy day; and we will forego the crops of the seventh year and the exaction of every debt. We also lay upon ourselves the obligation to charge ourselves yearly with the third part of a shekel for the service of the house of our God: for the showbread, the continual cereal offering, the continual burnt offering, the sabbaths, the new moons, the appointed feasts . . ." (Nehemiah 10, 29–33).

Some of the gravity with which the people took up this task of observing the Law can be seen further in the books of the Bible written during this late period. In the book of Nehemiah again we read that "when the people heard the law, they separated from Israel all those of foreign descent" (13, 3). And "in those days I saw in Judah men treading wine presses on the sabbath and bringing in heaps of grain and loading them on asses; and also, wine, grapes, figs, and all kinds of burdens, which they brought into Jerusalem on the sabbath day; and I warned them on the day when they sold food. Men of Tyre also, who lived in the city, brought in fish and all kinds of wares and sold them on the sabbath to the people of Judah and in Jerusalem. Then I remonstrated with the nobles of Judah and said to them, 'What is this evil thing which you are doing, profaning the sabbath day? Did not your fathers act in this way, and did not our God bring all this evil on us and on this city? Yet you bring more wrath upon Israel by profaning the sabbath' " (Nehemiah 13, 15–18) .

In the book of Daniel it is told of the youths taken off to Babylon at the time of the exile, that "the king assigned them a daily portion of the rich food which the king ate, and of the wine which he drank. . . . But Daniel resolved that he would not defile himself with the king's rich food or with the wine which he drank; therefore he asked the chief of the eunuchs to allow him not to defile himself" (1, 5. 8) . And when he received permission to try the experiment of eating only foods which would not defile himself, he and his companions lived for ten days on vegetables and water and "at the end of ten days it was seen that they were better in appearance and fatter in flesh than all the youths who ate the king's rich food. So the steward took away their rich food and the wine they were to drink, and gave them vegetables" (1, 15f.) .

The book of Judith is in the Greek bible but not in the Hebrew. It is considered "deuterocanonical" or "apocryphal" in the Catholic and Protestant bibles respectively. But it was a popular religious book of the Jewish people written in the time between the return from exile and the beginning of the Christian era. It reflects the mentality of those days regarding some of the points that interest us here.

When Judith went off on her mission to the enemy camp, she carried her own provisions: "She gave her maid a bottle of wine and a flask of oil, and filled a bag with parched grain and a cake of dried fruit and fine bread; and she wrapped up her vessels and gave them to her to carry" (Judith 10, 5) . (The vessels, too, from which one

26

ate had to be kept pure according to the Law. See Leviticus 10, 32–35, etc.)

Holofernes desired her to eat and drink with him: "Then he commanded them to bring her in where his silver dishes were kept, and ordered them to set a table for her with some of his own food and to serve her with his own wine. But Judith said, 'I cannot eat it, lest it be an offense. But I will be provided from the things I have brought with me.' Holofernes said to her, 'If your supply runs out, where can we get more like it for you? For none of your people is here with us.' Judith replied, 'As your soul lives, my lord, your servant will not use up the things I have with me before the Lord carries out by my hand what he has determined to do' " (Judith 12, 1–4).

Judith was also careful to perform the ritual washings necessary for perfect cleanliness. "She remained in the camp for three days, and went out each night to the valley of Bethulia, and bathed at the spring in the camp. . . . So she returned clean and stayed in the tent until she ate her food towards evening" (Judith 12, 5. 7).

But even when she was called in to Holofernes's presence: "to join us and eat and drink with us" (12, 11), and under orders to "please come to my lord and be honored in his presence and drink wine and be merry with us" (12, 13); "Drink now, and be merry with us!" (12, 17); and even when she answered "I will drink now, my lord. . . ."; still, "she took and ate and drank before him *what her maid had prepared*" (12, 19).

The book of Tobit, also from these post-exilic times, presupposes the same kind of concern in its pious narrator: "Now when I was carried away captive in Nineveh, all my brethren and my relatives ate the food of the Gentiles, but I kept myself from eating it, because I

27

remembered God with all my heart" (1, 10–12). The late (deuterocanonical) parts of the book of Esther show Esther appealing to the same separatist fidelity as evidence of piety: "And thy servant has not eaten at Haman's table, and I have not honored the king's feast or drunk the wine of the libations" (Esther 14, 17).

The books of Maccabees record the devotion which the revered saints and heroes of the nation had for these laws: "Many even from Israel gladly adopted his [the pagan king's] religion; they sacrificed to idols and profaned the sabbath. And the king sent letters by messengers to Jerusalem and the cities of Judah; he directed them to follow customs strange in the land, to forbid burnt offerings and sacrifices and drink-offerings in the sanctuary, to profane sabbaths and feasts, to defile the sanctuary and the priests, to build altars and sacred precincts and shrines for idols, to sacrifice swine and unclean animals, and to leave their sons uncircumcised. They were to make themselves abominable by everything unclean and profane so that they should forget the laws and change all the ordinances. 'And whoever does not obey the command of the king shall die'" (1 Maccabees 1, 43–50).

The persecutors are relentless against those who try to observe the Law: "According to the decree, they put to death the women who had had their children circumcised, and their families and those who circumcised them; and they hung the infants from their mothers' necks. But many in Israel stood firm and were resolved in their hearts not to eat unclean food. They chose to die rather than to be defiled by food or to profane the holy covenant; and they did die. And very great wrath came upon Israel" (1 Maccabees 1, 60–64).

The troubles just described provoke the Maccabean

rebellion. "They [the Jewish rebels] organized an army and struck down sinners in their anger and lawless men in their wrath. . . . they forcibly circumcised all the uncircumcised boys that they found within the borders of Israel" (1 Maccabees 2, 44.46).

The most outstanding examples of this sort of piety and zeal for the Law are found in 2 Maccabees, chapters 6 and 7. "A man could neither keep the sabbath nor observe the feasts of his fathers, nor so much as confess himself to be a Jew" (2 Maccabees 6, 6). "Two women were brought in for having circumcised their children. These women they publicly paraded about the city, with their babies hung at their breasts, then hurled them down headlong from the wall. Others who had assembled in the caves nearby, to observe the seventh day secretly, were betrayed to Philip and were all burned together, because their piety kept them from defending themselves, in view of their regard for that most holy day" (2 Maccabees 6, 10–11).

Then follows the story of the aged Eleazar, who "was being forced to open his mouth to eat swine's flesh. But he, welcoming death with honor, rather than life with pollution, went up to the rack of his own accord, spitting out the flesh, as men ought to do who have the courage to refuse things that it is not right to taste, even for the natural love of life" (2 Maccabees 6, 19–20). The persecutors try to persuade him at least to pretend that he has eaten swine's flesh, but he refuses lest he mislead younger men by the bad example of even such supposed compliance. Finally he is put to death by torture, "leaving in his death an example of nobility and a memorial of courage, not only to the young but to the great body of his nation" (2 Maccabees 6, 31).

The seventh chapter is the story of the mother and

her seven sons who "were being compelled by the king, under torture with whips and cords, to partake of unlawful swine's flesh" (2 Maccabees 7, 1). They are mutilated, flayed, burned alive, one after the other and the mother last of all, but they resist courageously.

These examples give us some true idea of how attached the people of those times were to the laws of sabbath observance, circumcision, and separatist purity in food and marriage. They are necessary background to any attempt to understand how shocking were such sayings of St. Paul as: "If you receive circumcision, Christ will be of no advantage to you" (Galatians 5, 2). "In Christ Jesus neither circumcision nor uncircumcision is of any avail, but faith working through love" (Galatians 5, 6). "You are severed from Christ, you who would be justified by the Law; you have fallen away from grace" (Galatians 5, 4). "You observe days and months and seasons and years! I am afraid I have labored over you in vain" (Galatians 4, 10).

"I know and am persuaded in the Lord Jesus that nothing is unclean in itself; but it is unclean for any one who thinks it unclean" (Romans 14, 14). "One man believes he may eat anything, while the weak man eats only vegetables. Let not him who eats despise him who abstains, and let not him who abstains pass judgment on him who eats . . . One man esteems one day as better than another, while another man esteems all days alike. Let everyone be fully convinced in his own mind. He who observes the day, observes it in honor of the Lord. He also who eats, eats in honor of the Lord, since he gives thanks to God; while he who abstains, abstains in honor of the Lord and gives thanks to God . . . Why do you pass judgment on your brother? Or why do you despise your brother?" (Romans 14, 1–3. 5–6. 10). "Food will not commend us to God. We are no worse off if we do not eat, and no better off if we do" (1 Corinthians 8, 8). "Eat whatever is sold in the marketplace without raising any question on the ground of conscience" (1 Corinthians 10, 25).

The revolutionary, impious sound of such statements against the background of faithful Judaism in the first century A.D. is obvious. <u>That which the people of God had held most holy is here being treated as unimportant.</u> Other New Testament material in this Pauline tradition states the case even more strongly:

"Let no one pass judgment on you in questions of food and drink or with regard to a festival or a new moon or a sabbath. These are only a shadow of what is to come; but the substance belongs to Christ" (Colossians 2, 16f.).

"If with Christ you died to the elemental spirits of the universe, why do you live as if you still belonged to the world? Why do you submit to regulations, 'Do not handle, Do not taste, Do not touch' (referring to things which all perish as they are used) according to human precepts and doctrines?" (Colossians 2, 20–22).

"Look out for the dogs, look out for the evil-workers, look out for those who mutilate the flesh. For we are the true circumcision, who worship God in spirit, and glory in Christ Jesus, and put no confidence in the flesh" (Philippians 3, 2f.).

"Now the Spirit expressly says that in later times some will depart from the faith by giving heed to deceitful spirits and doctrines of demons, through the pretensions of liars whose consciences are seared, who forbid marriage and enjoin abstinence from foods which God created to

31

be received with thanksgiving by those who believe and know the truth. For everything created by God is good and nothing is to be rejected if it is received with thanksgiving" (1 Timothy 4, 1–4).

These statements reject the practice of the Jewish Law for Christians—at least for Gentile Christians. They warn against the attempt of some to seduce Christians to take up the practice of the Law. Galatians is a severe reproach to Christian converts of Paul who have been tempted to adopt the practice of the Law.

All these statements about the Law, however, can be understood only in their historical context. It is a historical context in which that law was looked upon as God's own word to Israel, the most precious gift of God to men. It was looked upon as something worth dying for gladly. It was considered the most perfect way of showing one's love for God and faithfulness to him. This is the view of life which Paul so violently condemns in Galatians.

The anti-law traditions in the gospels do not seem to have been known in the Christian circles in which Paul moved. He never once (in this letter or in others) claims that Jesus of Nazareth taught we were liberated from the Law. He never once appeals to Jesus' example; for instance, Jesus' own violations of the sabbath or his criticism of the Jewish food laws (Mark 7, 15). Our tradition that Jesus himself opposed the Law is based on what we find in Mark 7 and in a modified form in Matthew 15. (Matthew prefers to stress "I am not come to destroy the Law" [5, 17] and "not one jot or tittle of the Law shall pass" [5, 18]). Luke-Acts relates that the apostles had no recollection at all of any such teaching on Jesus' part (see Acts 10; 11; 15).

Text and Paraphrase

1, 15 BUT WHEN THE ONE WHO HAD marked me out
and SET ME APART FROM MY VERY MOTHER'S WOMB
FINALLY THOUGHT IT GOOD—when he pleased, and
when his good time came—WHEN HE WHO HAD
1, 16 CALLED ME THROUGH HIS LOVING KINDNESS DECIDED
TO REVEAL HIS SON IN ME IN ORDER THAT I MIGHT
PREACH him and the good news about him, evangelizing HIM AMONG THE NATIONS, THEN I dropped all
that. I ADDED NOTHING AT ALL to what God then
revealed to me, AS A CONCESSION TO FLESH AND
BLOOD. For his word to me, his revealing, was not
in terms of flesh and blood. It had nothing to do
with external, fleshly observances. What he revealed
to me and what I set out to preach to the world
was purely and simply a message, a wonderful message, of salvation by belief in the loving, forgiving
goodness of God our Lord as shown in the cross
and resurrection of Christ.

Commentary

Christ brought a message of divine goodness, forgiveness,
and love. Christ himself became this message for all who
would believe in the proclaimed significance of his

cross. Salvation for men would consist precisely in believing what the cross and resurrection proclaimed. Man's very act of faith in the transforming reality of love, the saving power of God, the ultimate goodness of all that is and all that happens—this act of faith in the crucified Christ as risen, triumphant Lord of glory—would itself *be* the transformation of their personal lives. This belief would be their beginning of a new life. They would experience it as their own salvation.

Text and Paraphrase

1, 17 NOR DID I GO RUSHING UP TO JERUSALEM TO THOSE
WHO WERE APOSTLES BEFORE ME; I did not go to
the heads or messengers or preachers of the church
I had been persecuting. I knew that there was a
large and flourishing Christian community in our
capital city of Jerusalem, and that it was the oldest of all the Christian churches. But the rulers of
the church in Jerusalem had not given me the
message; God had. (I did not need them as sources
or authorities.) God and the insight he had given
me into the meaning of Christ and the reality of
Christ revealed in myself was my only authority,
my only source, my only justification. I planned
to join the already existing community of believing
Christians. I wanted to join them, meet them,
work and live in love with them. But still, the
insight I had received was especially directed to
my future life of spreading this good word among
the Gentiles, and so it was to the Gentiles I
headed. I WENT INSTEAD INTO ARABIA. AND THEN I
RETURNED ONCE MORE TO DAMASCUS.

possibly an overstatement

Commentary

Paul sought no permission to preach. He asked for no
instruction or clarification. He did not feel the need of
filling in background on the life of the historical Jesus
by consulting the eye-witnesses of that life. Nor did he
take the chance of letting himself be seen again by those
who had been his fellow persecutors. He avoided any risk
that they might now set upon him with fury as a traitor
and a heretic. He stayed away from all those he might
have known previously, and went off preaching on his
own in the region of Arabia. When things had quieted
down somewhat, he returned to Damascus. There is no
indication here of what many pious commentators suggest:
that Paul went off into "the desert of Arabia" in order to
meditate and pray in silence, and that there he might
gradually receive the fullness of God's revelation in prepa-
ration for this great mission. If Paul did go off to Arabia
for that purpose, the language he uses in verses 15 and 16
is very peculiar, for he would be saying: "When God, who
had set me apart for this from my mother's womb, finally
pleased to call me through his grace to reveal his son to me
in order that I might preach him among the Gentiles . . .
then, at that moment, I, instead of beginning to preach
him among the gentiles, went off to pray and meditate in
Arabia!"

Text and Paraphrase

1, 18 THEN AFTER THREE YEARS I DID FINALLY GO UP TO
JERUSALEM TO TELL MY STORY TO CEPHAS. I STAYED
1, 19 WITH HIM FOR TWO WEEKS. THE ONLY OTHER ONE OF
ALL THE APOSTLES in Jerusalem WHOM I DID SEE WAS
1, 20 JAMES, THE BROTHER OF THE LORD.—THESE THINGS I
AM WRITING TO YOU NOW, I swear BEFORE GOD THEY
ARE TRUE! That is the only contact with the Jerusalem church which I had. I never have claimed
more. I never have wanted more. Your faith, then,
my friends, did not come to you from the Jerusalem
church. It came from God through my word about
Jesus the Messiah. So do not let people say you
should correct that faith to correspond to what my
sources or my authorities supposedly hold, as if I
had human sources and authorities for what I have
preached and you have believed, because there have
been none. None! The point is so important that I
swear it before God as my witness!

Commentary

Cephas is the name Paul regularly uses for one of the
leading figures in the church of his day (see 2, 9–14). It
is a transliteration of the Aramaic word for rock. As the

gospel of John tells the story, it is the name given to the disciple Simon by Jesus: " 'You will be called Cephas,' which is translated Peter" (1, 42). The point of John's translation would, of course, be clear only to the Greek-speaking reader for whom John wrote, for Peter (*Petros*) is a man's name built out of the Greek word *"petra,"* rock. The name "Cephas" is translated by the name "Peter"; that is, the Aramaic word *"kepha"* means rock and so does the name "Peter" mean rock.

Paul, except for Galatians 2, 7f., always uses this Aramaic form of the name. Here he speaks of Cephas as of a person important enough that he himself made a visit to Jerusalem to see him and to tell him his story. Because of the later historical developments which culminated in today's papacy, the modern reader is interested in the role of Cephas (Peter) in early Christianity. A letter on Christian liberty might be expected to clarify somewhat the relationship of the Christian to those whom the "Holy Spirit has made overseers to give pasture to the church of God" (Acts 20, 28). One way to understand Cephas's role is to put together all the things said about him (under any of his names—Simon, Simon Peter, Peter, Cephas) in any part of the New Testament. Another way is to try to fit together not only all these New Testament statements and stories, but also all references to the same man in early literature, whether canonical or not. A third way is to look back from the later structures and traditions of the church and argue from the role of the men in the church who claim to be Peter's successors.

Here we want to follow none of these ways. We wish to try to understand Cephas only as Paul saw him; and for this understanding, if we want it to be solid and certain, we can safely appeal only to the letters of Paul himself (not to the later Acts of the Apostles). Here, in particular, we want to limit ourselves to the understanding of Cephas which can be gained from the letter to the Galatians. This is not to deny that the other sources of information have validity too. It is only to try to prevent several quite distinct sources of information from distorting and obscuring one another. The result of such a study then will not be the whole truth, but it will be one clear and definite piece of information: Peter's role in the church as knowable from Galatians. When we have finished (someday) studying the other sources in the same fashion, we will be able to set about asking in a reasonable way how the different sources fit together. Faith seems to encourage such a study, insofar as Galatians too was at one time examined and accepted by the Christian community as an inspired writing, "the word of God," while other similar ancient documents (the letter of Barnabas, the letters of Ignatius, and so forth) were rejected. There must be some sense in which Galatians in itself contains a valid and significant Christian insight. Since its theme is Christian freedom, its attitude to the question of authority in the church would seem worth examining.

Now who, according to Galatians, is Cephas? First of all, he seems to be someone whom Paul can presume his audience already had heard of. His name is introduced without explanation. He is someone in Jerusalem, and, together with James, the Lord's brother, he is one of the apostles in Jerusalem (v. 19: "I saw none of the other apostles, except James."). Cephas is then among "those who were apostles before me," whom Paul says he did not go up to Jerusalem to see (v. 17). Cephas

39

is one of those implied when Paul wrote, "I did not confer with flesh and blood" (v. 16).

In other words, Cephas is a leader in the Christian community in Jerusalem. Why does Paul go to see Cephas and tell him his story? Paul does not say. We cannot therefore presume at once that Cephas is "head of the church" and judge Paul's actions in the light of that presumption. "Head of the church" is of course a phrase which is never used for Peter or for anyone else but Christ in the entire New Testament. In fact, it is difficult to find in the New Testament any distinctive title for Peter. The First Epistle of Peter refers to him as "apostle of Jesus Christ" (1, 1), but many others bear this title. He is called "servant of Jesus Christ" (2 Peter 1, 1), but so are others (James 1, 1; Jude 1, 1). He is called "pillar" among others (Galatians 2, 9; Revelation 3, 12). He is *sumpresbuteros—fellow elder"* (1 Peter 5, 1), "witness" (1 Peter 5, 1), but neither are these proper to him alone.

Matthew 16, 18 says he is given the keys of the kingdom of heaven. This is distinctive, but it is not of itself a title, unless we should create for him the name "key-bearer." He is told that "whatever you bind on earth . . ." but, apart from the fact that the same statement is made to all the disciples (Matthew 18, 18), it again is not a title. Neither is there a title in the promise of Luke 22, 32: "I have prayed for you that your faith fail not, and that you, being once converted, confirm your brethren." "Shepherd" is implied but not stated in the commission to "feed my lambs, feed my sheep" of John 21, 15–17, but again this title is not distinctive of Peter, for it applies to other "overseers" in 1 Peter 5, 2; Acts 20, 28f. "Chief shepherd" (*archipoimēn*) on the other hand would seem apt, but it, like "head," happens to be reserved not to Peter but to Christ (1 Peter 5, 4; see "The Great Shepherd": Hebrews 13, 20).

The only distinctive title to express the pre-eminence of Peter to which many New Testament documents testify would seem to be his name itself, "Rock." Even this title, however, is not completely distinctive, for as used in Matthew 16, 18 it means rock on which the church is built, the foundation. But in Revelation 21, 14 the wall of the New Jerusalem has "twelve foundations [foundation stones] and on them twelve names of the twelve apostles of the lamb." And of course Christ for Paul in 1 Corinthians 3, 11 is "the foundation" and "other foundation no man can lay except that which has been placed, which is Jesus Christ."

Paul does not say why he goes to tell his story to Cephas, as distinguished from the other apostles (except James). But it is clear from what he does say that he thought it important to mention his visit to his readers. These people to whom Paul is writing have some high esteem for the Jerusalem church and presumably for its leaders, including Cephas. They seem to expect that Paul must have been authorized or commissioned by that church or by its leaders. And here he goes to great trouble to show and even to swear that he has received no such commission.

The people to whom Paul is writing had some special esteem—whether learned from Paul or from others who had come after him—for the original church, the mother church, at Jerusalem. He seems to feel they somehow expect that an argument can be settled by appealing to the practice and teaching of that mother church. Nor does Paul directly deny or attack those expectations.

Instead, he shows that he was in good relationship with the mother church and its leaders. He had spoken with Cephas and explained his own story to him. All he denies is dependence. He says he spoke with Cephas only once during a single visit of fifteen days, and this three years after his own conversion and divine commission to the apostolate.

Whether that visit had been "official" or private Paul does not say, but he also indicates that he did not come to Jerusalem to learn from the apostles there. The only ones he met were Cephas and James, the brother of the Lord. (This James is not ordinarily reckoned one of the original twelve.) He came, he says, to report, to "tell his story" to Cephas.

Is it perhaps implied in this special mention of Cephas that Paul and his readers knew that Cephas was "the Rock" upon whom the entire Christian church was founded, as later tradition read Matthew 16, 18—"upon this Rock I will build my church"? That is hard to say; first of all because it is doubtful whether Paul had any conception of "the church" as a single world-wide organization. He uses the word "church" for the individual churches, the local assemblies, gatherings, groups of Christians in individual towns and houses. There is the church of Prisca's house (1 Corinthians 16, 19) and the church of Philemon's house (Philemon 2) and the churches of the region of Galatia (Galatians 1, 2). "Church" is almost certainly not even the right word for us to use in translating his Greek word *"ekklesia."* For our word "church" is already so laden with sacral connotations, so removed from everyday life, so religious and mystical, that we miss the fact that Paul's word would have first struck his Greek-speaking readers as a word taken from everyday experience in normal secular life. It meant group, gathering, meeting, assembly, congregation, convocation. In this sense they would have understood it first as referring to the little group which could meet at one time in the house of one member of the community. Thus a large city could have many "churches," just as it could have many "bishops" as their supervisors ("*episkopoi*" —Acts 20, 28).

In the letters of Paul which are certainly genuine there is no statement about "the church" which could not be better translated "the assembly" and be understood as referring to the gathering of the group of believers in an ordinary house to pray and reflect together. But "the gathering," the group, could also easily refer (as in modern languages) to that collection of persons who came together *regularly*. In this extended sense, "the gathering" could refer not only to this gathering here at Chloe's house and that group which met there at Prisca's and Aquila's house (Romans 16, 3–5), but also to all believers everywhere, "the gathering" much like "the gathering of Israel"—a term used also in the Old Testament and soon picked up by the Christians. This "gathering" (our "universal church") occurs in the late letters, Ephesians and Colossians, where there is discussion of the mystical, spiritual reality of "the gathering" under the image of "the body of Christ." But even in Colossians the other and more fundamental usage recurs: "Nympha and the church in her house" (Colossians 4, 15).

Thus it would be hard to imagine that Paul asked himself whether someone was the rock on which the church was built, whose "keys to the kingdom of heaven" empowered him to direct and govern the whole body of the faithful. In his time there was no organized "universal church" to be governed, nor anything much for the "universal church," as a body spread over the earth, to do. There was the task of believing the gospel and of living in love and service according to the gospel. But that would probably not have needed orders from above then, any more than it needs them today. Where the need for a single leader is particularly felt is where united action for a single goal is desired, where serious disputes as to courses of action or as to belief arise, where uniformity is desired, where quick communication and/or a shortcut to mutual recognition is needed. United action of Christians for a particular earthly goal did not arise as a possibility or necessity in the literature of that age so far as we know it. Serious disputes did arise, and Galatians treats of one of these and tells something of how it was handled. Uniformity seems not to have been either their concern or ideal except in solicitude for preaching one true gospel. Communication and recognition do not seem to have been major problems, at least of any sort which could have been facilitated by working through a single central office.

Still, Paul did address himself on this visit to Cephas rather than to the community as a whole, or to the whole group of its "important-seeming ones" (2, 6), its "pillars" (2, 9). This is strange in light of the fact that James's name is placed ahead of Cephas's in 2, 9. (Who today would speak of having visited Rome and presented his case before "Seper, Paul VI and Antoniutti"?) Perhaps Paul and his readers knew that Cephas had some special interest or concern for the churches outside of Jerusalem. Perhaps this is the concern referred to in 2, 7f.—that Peter personally had been "confided the gospel for the circumcised," that Christ's spirit worked in some special way in Peter for the apostolate among the Jews.

If Paul did mention his visit to Peter because he somehow knew that the Rock was generally considered responsible for the churches outside Jerusalem, then it is important for our understanding of church order to know what Paul definitely does *not* do. Paul does not expect the Rock to be the initiator of all movements in the church. He does not come to him asking to be given a mission. He does not even, so far as he tells us, ask for any formal blessing on his work. He tells Cephas his story. He tells him what he has been doing. He keeps him informed as to what is going on in other Christian churches, under the inspiration and guidance of the Spirit. Why? One good reason would be: if Peter was indeed the Rock on which Christ wished his church to be built, it would be good to keep Peter informed of what was going on in the church. Such information might help him be a foundation and center of the church's unity. He could support the action of the Spirit when he heard about it, he might encourage Paul who was laboring in the Spirit for the growth of the church, and he might possibly encourage and exhort others to follow Paul's example, to take up similar work to help what Paul—or the Spirit through Paul—has already begun.

Paul does not expect Cephas to answer questions for him about how the work is to be done. He makes no special effort to tap this rock as some unique source of the waters of truth. Perhaps he thought that his regard for Peter as foundation and center of unity, as support for the church and the activity of the Spirit in the whole church, was quite sufficient.

45

We shall not even discuss the fact that Paul clearly does not expect the Rock to play the role of suppressing, of crushing, the action the Spirit has begun through him. Nor need we discuss what would have been Paul's reaction if Cephas had attempted anything of that sort towards him.

Now it is true, the Christian of a later age always tends to set Paul apart as someone in a situation completely different from his own. Paul, he thinks, could act in so daring a way because Paul *knew* God had revealed a special mission to him, while we of a later age can never be sure whether our inspirations are from God. Still, any serious study of the prophetic phenomenon in the general history of religions will reveal that those who claim to have received a message from heaven are always personally convinced of the authenticity of their message. And yet, that very conviction is always—and necessarily —to some extent an act of faith on their part. On reflection (to which external circumstances often force them or those who follow them) it becomes clear that for them as for any other mortal, it is impossible to *know* that God has spoken to oneself. You may be certain as certain can be that your message represents God's will and that he has brought you to an understanding of the message—but that certainty is still an act of faith. Your conviction that this comes from God and not from your own insight or imagination is an act of faith. Your recognition that the outside influence you think you feel in yourself is of divine origin, rather than diabolic, psychological, telepathic, extra-terrestrial, cannot possibly rest on evidence. It must be an act of faith.

There is no reason to think Paul was not subject to this same universal religious phenomenon. Only madmen are certainly exempt from it. But this means Paul's case was not—experientially, as experienced by Paul himself—essentially different from what might happen in the life of any later Christian. One might feel a call from God. One might be sure it was God speaking to him, calling to him. What this feels like, I don't know. But many men have testified to the feeling. When it occurs, the individual who experiences it is the only one in the world who can make the judgment of recognition: is this God and from God or is it not? And the obligation to make that judgment is upon him. He must make it. He cannot escape it. Either he decides the message is not of God, and therefore can be ignored. Or he decides it is of God and therefore must be followed no matter who stands in the way.

Even such considerations as: "God works through established channels" or "God will not tell us to go contrary to his appointed representatives and authorities"—even these will not justify a person's avoiding the crucial decision when he once feels or thinks he feels the hand of God upon him. For in a case like Paul's, for example, God precisely did *not* work through established channels, either Christian or Jewish, and God *did*, in the act of Paul's conversion, very much and very directly go against his appointed representatives: for he told Paul to go against his own lifelong fidelity to the appointed and established authorities of Judaism, who were persecuting the Christians. He told Paul to go against, to renounce for himself, obedience to the established authority which was the Law. But these were the only established authorities Paul had known up till then. To respond, "But God had already rejected those authorities, to set up new ones in their place," is simply to beg the question. No one involved in the events of the time could possibly have known what God had decided. In fact, our "knowing" it is only a way of saying that we are believing Catholic Christians. A Jew of today, for instance, like many Christians of Paul's time, would not see any justification for claiming that the old authorities have been abrogated by God.

Text and Paraphrase

1, 21 AFTER THAT I WENT TO THE REGIONS OF SYRIA
1, 22 AND TO CILICIA. I WAS ABSOLUTELY UNKNOWN BY
SIGHT TO THE CHURCHES OF JUDEA WHICH ARE IN
CHRIST.

Commentary

Note that, were we to judge from this letter alone, we
would have to conclude that Paul had never visited Jerusalem at all before this. The Paul who is described in the
much later Acts of the Apostles, on the other hand,
would have had to be well known in Jerusalem. He had
studied there "at the feet of Gamaliel" (Acts 22, 3). He
had stood by approvingly at the stoning of Stephen in
Jerusalem, and the witnesses to that crime had laid their
garments at his feet (Acts 7, 58; 8, 1). He had persecuted
the church in Jerusalem from house to house, dragging
out men and women and throwing them into prison
(Acts 8, 3). None of this fits very well with "I was absolutely unknown by sight to the churches of Judea." The
Paul who describes himself in this letter to the Galatians
does not mention where his earlier career was spent. We
know he had been in Damascus before his conversion or
at the time of it because he says in 1, 17 that he "re-

49

turned again" or "turned back again to Damascus." At
the same time, when he mentions Jerusalem for the first
time in this letter (also in 1, 17) he does not say he
returned there but simply that "I went up to Jerusalem."

Text and Paraphrase

1, 23 THEY ONLY HEARD OF ME THAT "HE WHO ONCE
PERSECUTED US IS NOW preaching the message, the
good news, is now EVANGELIZING THE FAITH HE
1, 24 ONCE ABUSED." AND THEY GLORIFIED GOD IN ME. THEN
2, 1 AFTER FOURTEEN MORE YEARS, I WENT UP TO JERU-
SALEM FOR THE SECOND TIME. I traveled WITH
BARNABAS, my friend and Jewish brother, TAKING
ALONG TITUS AS WELL, a Gentile, and my convert.
2, 2 NOW I WENT UP ACCORDING TO REVELATION—not
"according to man" (1, 11). For my gospel is not
according to man or man's ideas. I went up in the
spirit in which I had been living and preaching all
those years; in the spirit of liberty, in the spirit of
disclosing Jesus as Messiah, according to the dis-
closure which had been made to me and in me.
AND I PUT UP TO THEM THE GOSPEL THAT I PREACH
AMONG THE NATIONS; AND IN PARTICULAR I PUT IT TO
THOSE WHO SEEMED IMPOSING. I'm telling you all
this now LEST you imagine or claim SOMEHOW I AM
RUNNING OR WAS RUNNING THEN TO NO PURPOSE.

Commentary

Thus Paul came to make his report to "ecclesiastical authority" or what may have come closest to ecclesiastical

51

authority in the church of his day. He came after seventeen years—or, since he had also once made a short two-week visit, let us say he came to report more in detail and settle a few questions after fourteen years. During those fourteen or seventeen years apparently he had reported to no one. As explained above, he seems to have felt no need to submit to human judgment a divine inspiration.

Why exactly did he finally make this visit then? Most probably because some troubles were already developing of the sort which are behind this whole letter. Certainly the Jew-Gentile problem was among those discussed on this visit (see vv. 3 and 9). But Paul is not intent here on telling us why he made the visit or even all that was accomplished during it. He is intent on one thing alone: making the essential point that he did not receive his gospel from the first apostles, the group centered in Jerusalem. If there was any dependence or borrowing, it would seem from this verse it must have been the other way around. He explained the gospel to them as he saw it.

There is an interesting possibility of church order implied here. Paul, remaining free and independent in the Spirit, does explain in the presence of those "who seemed imposing" what he has been preaching. Why? That they might pass judgment on it? Everything in the context indicates the opposite. That they might tell him perhaps he was wrong and should stop? Everything in the letter so far indicates that was out of the question. When he says "lest I am running or was running then to no purpose," he is not implying that he was not sure of his course before he told the authorities about it. The whole thrust of his argument is in the

52

opposite direction. Besides, how could a reasonable man have preached something as the heart of his gospel for *fourteen years* without asking for confirmation, if he really believed such confirmation was necessary?

No, he must mean: "I am telling you about my meeting with them so that you do not have doubts about whether I was running ('doing my work as an apostle' —see 1 Corinthians 9, 24ff.) to no purpose." And he may mean too, "lest they or anyone else continue working in a direction opposed to mine, in such a way that all my labor be frustrated by their counter-labor, and vice-versa." As Paul says in 4, 11 to the Galatians themselves after reflecting on how they are following after other teachers: "I fear that I have labored among you to no purpose."

What seems to be going on is this: There were Christian communities at a very early date all over the land which today makes up the state of Israel, that is, in the territories which then were Judea, Samaria and Galilee. But the most important of these was in the city of Jerusalem itself where the Lord had taught and especially where he suffered and died. The historical causes and occasions of the importance cannot be sorted out: the fact of the Lord's death and resurrection in that city; the charge to the first apostles, reported in Luke-Acts, to remain there and the first manifestation of the Spirit (also only in Luke-Acts) in Jerusalem on Pentecost; the pre-eminence of Jerusalem in the history and prophecy (and apocalyptic?) of Israel; the political importance of Jerusalem in the first century.

At any rate, Jerusalem was in fact outstanding among the earliest communities and had the reputation of having been the first full-sized Christian community in the world. Consequently, it would have been normal to ask a new preacher whether when he said "Christ" he meant the same thing by his preaching as the earliest disciples had meant back in Jerusalem. And as an indication that he did, he might well be expected to give some evidence that he was a brother and recognized as a brother in Christ by that original Christian community. Paul will speak of "the right hand of fellowship" (2, 9) and the word "fellowship—communion—community: *koinōnia*" becomes a technical term. One asks whether this or that person, this or that church, this person and that church, are "in communion" with one another. Here the question is whether Paul is in communion with Jerusalem.

The letter implies the Galatians were interested in the question. They probably had not picked it up as a consideration or problem from Paul. It is more likely that the idea was raised in their minds by those who came to them promoting observance of the Law of Moses. Not that these people necessarily came to teach them to be subject to the church at Jerusalem or to the apostles who taught there. The Law did not make Jews of the diaspora subject to the elders of Jerusalem either. The main concerns of these people who were promoting legal observance in Galatia were doctrinal. Their concern was the "full message" of Christianity—as they saw it. For them that message included life according to the law given to Israel. And as the arguments waxed warm over the "real" meaning of the faith both sides professed, it would have been a natural step for those who favored the Law to appeal to the practice and belief of the mother church as surely correct and as somehow, at least because earlier, authoritative for all. In a not dissimilar way, Paul himself makes appeal in one of his letters to what "we teach in all the churches" (1 Corinthians 4, 17) and to the fact that (in regard to women speaking in the assembly) "we have no such custom, nor do the churches of God" (1 Corinthians 11, 16).

Now they may not have intended their appeal to the custom of Jerusalem to be a demand to subject the Galatians to Jerusalem as to a ruling authority. They may simply have believed their own doctrine and practice was truly indispensable, and been intent on supporting it by any argument or any pressure they could find. The practice and belief of Jerusalem was a handy argument and weapon for their purpose. (Others would later appeal in similar circumstances to the belief and practice of the ancient and honorable and powerful church at Rome.) They may, as part of their argument, have claimed further that the Jerusalem apostles were for one reason or another superior to Paul. (Certainly Paul's adversaries in other places, notably in Corinth, did this.)

But whatever their exact intention, their appeal to Jerusalem as normative would in practice have been a step in the direction of accepting a central authority in the church as a whole, a human authority which could decide on the truth and falsity, rightness or wrongness of a teaching or practice, at least in the light of continued tradition and past practice. Thus if Paul and his followers submit to these arguments and appeals, one norm of rightness will grow up and be on its way towards being accepted universally—the norm of what the principal, leading, or oldest church decides. And once this begins, the universal, united, the one "catholic" church is under way.

Now such a universal and united church, with its possibilities of definitive decisions reached by common agreement of submission to one central authority, has certain decided administrative advantages, in any age. Paul does not deny that it is a possible line of development for the local churches if they want to develop their universal and united aspects; if they want to proceed further along the road of union. But he still asserts his own independence from anybody's decision or command in regard to what he preaches. With that point established earlier in the letter, he here nevertheless goes on to explore the possibilities of showing that for all his independence, he had been and had remained in communion with the Jerusalem church, and this in spite of an important difference with them in regard to both doctrine and practice.

It is the notion then of "*koinōnia,* communion" which needs further reflection. If the Christian churches were in communion with each other, recognized each other as fellow believers and sufferers in the Lord, the universal church would seem to have all the unity essential to it, a true and conscious, recognized brotherhood of believers throughout the world. And as the number of churches multiplied, and it became less practical and desirable for every Christian church in every city of the world to investigate the credentials of every other church in the world, it surely was natural to take the expedient of simply admitting communion with all churches which were themselves in communion with one or the other of the better known and major churches. One such church then, perhaps for a long time the only one, was the Jerusalem church. Preachers and churches which were in communion with her were automatically in communion with one another. It would be a quick way of establishing or affirming or reassuring unity among many diverse parties and churches. That one church, which all use in order to assure their communion with one another, would automatically become the central church for a region, perhaps for all Christendom. This makes the role of central church or mother church intelligible, even in a theology like Paul's, where commands in the strict sense from headquarters are unjustifiable; even in an age like his where no world-wide projects are being undertaken or world-wide conformity being pursued.

But it cannot be stressed too much that being in communion with another person or church does not mean being subject and having to obey him or it. That is abundantly clear from Paul's words here and elsewhere. Nor would communion mean necessarily believing and practicing all that the other church or person believes and practices. For instance, Paul and Jerusalem obviously did not share the same belief and practice on some very important points. Communion would mean only admitting publicly that one recognizes the other's beliefs and practices as basically christian, at least in their motivation; and that one's own beliefs and practices are similarly recognized by the other in his turn. This much of a sharing, a community, there would have had to be between the Jerusalem church and any other which was to be in communion with it, or with which it wanted to be in communion. (The mutuality of communion is important.)

But none of this would mean—necessarily—that those in communion were subject to Jerusalem, nor that they looked identical with Jerusalem in teaching and practice. There need be agreement only on the heart of the gospel, the kerygma: Christ suffered and died and rose from the dead, and this is our salvation. All who believe that and who believe life should be lived in accordance with that in love and sacrifice recognize one another's Christianity. They feel bound in love to one another, they encourage and exhort one another to the fullness of the difficult life such a faith demands. They receive one another and envoys from one another as true brothers. They are willing to pray together and eat together (eucharist).

To a Catholic, trained in a more directly authoritarian position, it may seem that if Paul is not obliged to submit his gospel to the judgment of the mother church, then Jerusalem and its apostolic college had nothing special to their credit except a certain honor and dignity. But there is no valid reason for thinking that the medieval canonists' distinction between "primacy of honor" and "primacy of jurisdiction" exhausts the entire range of possibilities. It is a very real thing that the church should have a center. It could be very real and very useful and very important that there should be a place where different tendencies and even opposing tendencies can be brought into confrontation with one another lest either side "labor in vain" and to cross-purposes. It is valuable that there should be a place in the church where each one can speak freely of the gospel as God has revealed it to him, and can still testify to his sense of unity with others whose approach may be different and sometimes even contradictory. It is good that when many and large parties are involved in discussions they should have a shortcut to indicate their basic agreement with one another: the simple device of saying "I am in union with the mother church at Jerusalem. Are you? Then we are brothers." There should always be in the church an external sign and symbol of unity to which appeal can be made and which can help hold differing groups together at least in practical activity, general aims of helping and bettering the lot of their fellow man, showing forth love in the world, and finally showing love in practice towards one another.

All of this is implied as a possibility in Paul's making an effort, when questions arose, to put his gospel up to the Jerusalem church and especially to those who seemed important in it—even though he had not the slightest doubt about his gospel, and was in no way ready to give it up or change it ("If I or an angel from heaven preach to you another gospel from the one you have received, let him go to hell"—1, 8).

2, 3 BUT not at all! When I put it directly to them, why NOT EVEN TITUS WHO WAS WITH ME—AND WHO WAS known to be A GREEK!—WAS REQUIRED TO BE CIRCUMCISED. So they heard me, seventeen years after my conversion and after I had begun preaching Christ, finally tell them in detail how I conceived the gospel for the Gentiles. They heard, and found nothing at all to object to in the things I said. They knew I was not ordering the Gentiles to be circumcised, much less to obey the other detailed things commanded in the law of Moses. They saw me traveling with Titus, an uncircumcised Gentile. They saw me calling him brother; eating with him. And they made no objection.

2, 4 AND now is all this to change ON ACCOUNT OF SOME DRAGGED-IN FALSE BRETHREN WHO HAVE COME SLIPPING INTO OUR MIDST IN ORDER TO TAKE SUPERVISORY CHARGE OVER OUR LIBERTY, THE LIBERTY WE HAVE IN CHRIST JESUS, IN ORDER TO MAKE US THEIR SLAVES? Now shall such requirements be imposed on them, on us, on you, because of the likes of them?!

2, 5 Hah! TO SUCH PERSONS WE HAVE NEVER YIELDED ANY SUBMISSION, NOT EVEN FOR A MOMENT, but rather have always resisted boldly IN ORDER THAT THE TRUTH OF THE GOSPEL MIGHT ABIDE and might continue ALL THE WAY DOWN TO YOU. Shall I then, after the boldness I showed in exposing my gospel simple and entire to the great Jerusalem apostles, now quake in the face of these late-comers, these false brethren who have shown up but recently? After the respect and fine reception received from the great Jerusalem apostles, shall I now pay attention to the quibbling objections of men like these who have come upon you now?

God knows where they came from or who dragged them in to adduce false testimony against me! Certainly I will not pay any attention to their attacks. Let them look to themselves. They want to come in now and play bishop over us (*kataskopeō* for *episkopeō*); they want to be supervisors over our liberty? Certainly not! That liberty from the rule of law is the liberty we have in Christ. Abandon that, and you abandon the essential: the rule over us of the one law of love and sacrifice which is implied in our faith in him as Lord.

Why do they want to do that to us? Because they want power, rule. They want to set up again a system like that of the old religion where there were appointed guardians of truth who must be consulted as to the Law's real meaning. They hope again for a system where men cannot decide for themselves, but must crawl to experts on the Law for interpretations and exemptions and permissions before they can cook and eat, wash and dress, live and love, sing and pray, breathe and sleep. That is why I call these men false brethren. I don't know their hearts. They may have the best intentions in the world. But in fact they are calling for

61

a return to a system where they or others like them will play the lord, burden men's consciences with new rules and laws in place of the old, and then sit in judgment on those agonized consciences and sell relief at the expense of independence, of individuality, of personality, of manhood.

Commentary

But Paul resists—first "that the gospel may stand," at least in his own day. And then Paul resists in order that the gospel and all it implies may be recorded in its purity in this letter, in a letter which, in God's providence, the church will recognize as sacred scripture, so that some day in some future age, no matter how many corrupters may have crept in and perverted the truth in practice in the meantime, men's eyes might again be opened to its truth; so that God's call in Christ might be heard clearly; in order, as he says, "that the truth of the gospel might come down"—no matter over how many centuries of intervening time—"even unto you."

And so it has. The other system, the thought of which angers Paul, is a system to which men in their weakness unfortunately will always tend. Not only the natural lust for power and dominance on the part of those who hope to lead brings this about. It is just as much caused by the natural weakness on the part of the others, the majority, those who will end up dominated, imposed upon, serving and obeying. It is, in this latter case, a manifestation of that fatal weakness in men by which they prefer not to have to make decisions, not to have to bear full responsibility for their own actions and judgments. This is the weakness so perfectly sketched by Dostoevsky in the story of the grand inquisitor. Men rise up in the face of this weakness, to play the overseer (*episkopos*, bishop) as a concession to their fellow men; even as a service. Let the weak pass off responsibility to a select few who will bear its awful burden! Religion has always offered this possibility to men to some extent. All organization and institution does it in some measure. But true Christianity, with its frightening message of faith and its constant demand for free faith given daily, given almost from moment to moment, deprives men of this support. A basic craving remains unsatisfied. An instinctive tendency of religious psychology continues to exert its drive; and the little flock of Christians begins to fall into the system of order, of law, of obedience, of institutionalization against which Paul warns so vigorously here.

As they do so, they lose that which is most distinctively their own as Christians. The fundamental driving principle of one's life cannot at one same moment be both law and faith. The fundamental core virtue cannot be simultaneously obedience and responsible decision. Because the weaknesses described are so deep-seated in human nature, the problem of resisting them will be a perennial problem. But in a church which is to last till the end of the world, it is a problem which will always be faced boldly. Some ages may yield more to these temptations than others. But they will always be succeeded by other ages which reinstitute Pauline reforms. Paul's words, "How quickly you have transferred over to another gospel," will always be a significant warning, and always necessary. And no matter how many years have preceded any individual fall from the high ideal he proposes, the true church of Christ will always, from the depths of her sincere repentance, look on her sin as having been an over-hasty fall from Christ's true ideal, she will always be shocked that it ever happened to her at all, and she will undertake an immediate movement toward recovery.

In the eyes of those who see this truth, the ones who would help oppose the truth and warp it will always seem "false brethren." It will always be necessary to warn the rest of the church against them, even when they play this supervisory role from the chair of an official supervisor (as Paul will illustrate in the next paragraph). One who sounds such warnings will, of course, be a troublemaker in the eyes of the authorities he is opposing. As the authorities or would-be authorities see their own efforts, they themselves are only strengthening the church of Christ, arranging all things in good order; easing consciences by enlightening them as well as by helping free them from the agony of decision. The man who like Paul opposes this, well-intentioned and "prophetic" though he may think himself, must be prepared to suffer at their hands for the gospel.

Those who claim to be defending the authority-principle against such a critic will say of him: "The values of the church Christ founded must be preserved. The good of the institution, of the many, comes before the good of any private individual. This institution is the church, the body of Christ. Law, order, direction, obedience, subordination, organization—all these help her and so we provide them." In the face of this, the man who takes Paul's warning seriously must cling in faith to his realization that the gospel is above all else a call, a challenge, and a promise to the individual, not a blue-print for an institution. He must remain true to the insight that the church is a very special kind of society and institution

—one whose whole purpose of existence is the good of individual human beings, of persons. The conflict, "individual vs. institution," "person vs. community," can never really arise in the church. It may seem to arise—but that is only because the church is never living up to the fullness of being which Christ planned for her. Ideally, the organization which is the church will always be ready to sacrifice itself for the good of any individual. Doing so, it will be most like Christ—will be most truly the Body of Christ in this world. And in this way, sacrificing itself in faith through love, the church will always, like Christ, rise from its grave to glorious new life.

Every Christian who cares for the church—and so, above all, those who are called by their office to care for the church—must repeat in faith the words of faith Christ speaks in the gospel: "the gates of hell will not prevail against her"; "I am with you all days, even to the consummation of the world." This will be his gift to a church which believes and lives by his word. In no text of the gospel however is the church cautioned to watch out for herself in order to preserve herself by careful human planning, by administration and organization, banking, property and political alliances. These are tools of human wisdom; but when Christ speaks of the church enduring through the ages, he makes a promise of faith to faith. He says *he* will preserve the church. We, the disciples, are to take no thought for tomorrow. We are to sell all we have and give it away; we are to fear not, for the Father has disposed unto us a kingdom. He does not ask us to preserve the church. Indeed, it would seem he rather assures us we cannot do so even if we wish. As a matter of fact, the frequent attempts made to preserve the church by strengthening her human organizational tech-

65

niques seem a proof of this. They seem to show that the more men do try to preserve the church in any way but by their own living in faith and attempting to preach the faith to others, so much the more do they make the church less a church, less the body of Christ on earth, and less an instrument of men's sanctification and salvation.

Text and Paraphrase

2, 6   AND FROM THOSE WHO SEEMED TO BE SOMETHING IMPORTANT—WHAT KIND OF MEN THEY ONCE WERE MAKES NO DIFFERENCE TO ME, (as I would hope that what kind of man I was once would make no difference to them or to you) FOR GOD DOES NOT LOOK AT THE FACE OF MEN, is no respecter of persons —NOW THESE IMPORTANT-SEEMING PEOPLE THEM-SELVES ADDED NOTHING FURTHER to my gospel or my preaching or my understanding of the message of Christ—just as I said above that I had tried with such great care never to add anything to it over and above the message itself: salvation through faith in his cross and resurrection.

2, 7   RATHER, QUITE TO THE CONTRARY, SEEING THAT I HAD BEEN ENTRUSTED WITH THE GOOD NEWS OF THE UNCIRCUMCISED JUST AS PETER HAD BEEN WITH THAT

2, 8   OF THE CIRCUMCISED, (FOR HE WHO HAD WORKED IN PETER FOR THE APOSTOLATE OF THE JEWS, WAS

2, 9   WORKING IN ME TOO FOR THE GENTILES) AND KNOW-ING THE GIFT WHICH HAD BEEN GIVEN ME, JAMES AND CEPHAS AND JOHN, THOSE WHO SEEMED TO BE THE PILLARS, GAVE ME AND BARNABAS RIGHT HANDS OF FELLOWSHIP, SO THAT WE SHOULD GO TO THE GENTILES, AND THEY TO THE CIRCUMCISED. This was our characteristically Christian solution: let the other party alone. Each side practice in peace what each truly believes (see Romans 14, 1–11). And, in telling how we came to this solution, I hope I have made it clear to my opponents among you that if they want to put stock in appeals to authority (useless though such appeals are), I am quite as well equipped with the recognition, authorization of "church-officials" and especially of the twelve apostles of Jerusalem as any man on earth. If the first apostles themselves agreed I should preach to the Gentiles and they to the Jews, then how can anyone be coming in to disturb you Galatians with charges supposedly representing apostolic opinions and teachings as opposed to mine?

2, 10   They asked ONLY THAT WE SHOULD BE MINDFUL OF THE POOR: THE VERY THING WHICH I MYSELF WAS

2, 11   EAGER TO DO. AND WHEN CEPHAS CAME TO ANTIOCH —you may never have heard of the occasion, but I can never forget it. You all know Antioch, at any rate—the city which has become a sort of capital for the non-Jewish branch of Christianity—I TOOK MY STAND AGAINST HIM, TO THIS VERY FACE, BECAUSE HE WAS FULLY DESERVING OF CONDEMNATION. Why?

2, 12   Well, BECAUSE BEFORE SOME MEN CAME FROM JAMES, HE HAD BEEN EATING WITH THE GENTILES BUT WHEN THEY CAME, HE WITHDREW AND SEPARATED HIMSELF, FEARING THOSE OF THE CIRCUMCISION.

Commentary

So it is the same problem: the obligation of the Jewish laws on purity and cleanliness in eating, the separatism implied in those laws, and, as a result, the overall problem of the obligation of Christians to observe the law of Moses. Cephas was Jewish; Paul was Jewish. But, at least in the Gentile capital of Antioch, both mingled freely with the Gentiles and ate with them and lived with them as brothers. In Jerusalem Cephas, as one of the leaders and a member of the original apostolic group, had lived as did the other Christians in Jerusalem, observing the Law. But even there, he and the other apostles—including James—had not imposed the restrictions of the Law on the Gentile Titus and had not insisted that Paul change in any way his preaching of the gospel of freedom to the Gentiles.

But during this stay of Peter in Antioch, more Jews arrived from Jerusalem—emissaries of James, who was with Cephas one of the pillars. As soon as they came, Peter changed his practice. Did the men from James ask him to change? Did they accuse him of sin? Did they accuse him of disloyalty? Did they threaten him with public exposure back home for his living outside the Law among the Gentiles in Antioch? We do not know. It may have been that the decision was entirely Peter's own, and based merely on a fear of what these visitors might think. Perhaps he never discussed the subject with them or with anyone else.

He knew that they were strict observers of the Law themselves. He knew that according to the strict terms of the Law, what he was doing was forbidden. The Law would call him a sinner. God's law did not permit his free mingling and eating with Gentiles, that was all there was to it. Great Jewish heroes of the near past had given their lives, he would remember, for clinging to these seemingly trivial regulations out of loyalty to their people and their God.

Perhaps then Cephas simply feared the possibility of the accusations that might be made against him. Perhaps he trembled before the mere thought that these defenders of the law of God might stand before him in open community and charge him with being a sinner. Nothing indicates exactly why these men came "from James"—whether they were in Antioch merely on a visit; or whether they were making what the later church would call a "visitation," investigating living conditions in Antioch, checking for instance whether Paul was indeed limiting his apostolate to the Gentiles there and leaving what Jews there were in Antioch to the supervision of the Jerusalem apostles. The voice, then, of tradition and of law spoke out—whether openly or only in Peter's troubled imagination. Whatever the details of the actual event, we know at least what Paul tells us—that Cephas had been living with the Antioch church quite freely; but when the visitors appeared, he shifted back to observance of the Law and consequently withdrew from the Gentile part of the Antioch community.

Text and Paraphrase

2, 13 AND THE REST OF THE JEWS JOINED HIM IN HIS
HYPOCRISY, SO THAT EVEN BARNABAS WAS DRAWN OVER
INTO THEIR HYPOCRISY.

Commentary

This is the normal reaction to pressure from "authority,"
"tradition," and "law." Even where the pressure has not
been exerted, but is only feared as probable or possible,
the same reaction is likely to occur. No one likes the
possibility of being left standing alone—the last, lonely
defender of a cause from which the others have safely
withdrawn. And so here even Paul's friend and companion
Barnabas was being pulled along and the rest of the
Jewish members of the community with him. In other
words, Paul probably was left entirely alone, except for
the Gentiles, whose status was precisely in question. If
Paul was to raise his voice against this shift back into
legalism, into the way of law, obedience and submission,
he would have to do so out of his inner resources of
courage and faith and nothing else besides. He knew
he was defending the truth. But looking around for some
confirmation or support from outside himself, he found
none whatsoever. The representatives of tradition stood

against him. The waverers and doubters, the time-servers, the followers, and all who preferred obedience to personal decision stood against him. And the Law itself most clearly stood against him. But Paul was convinced he had the true revelation of God's love in Christ and the true understanding of what that meant for man's living. And so he spoke out.

Text and Paraphrase

2, 14 AND WHEN I SAW THEY WERE NOT WALKING STRAIGHT
IN THE DIRECTION OF THE TRUTH OF THE GOSPEL, I
SAID TO CEPHAS IN FRONT OF THEM ALL: IF YOU,
WHO ARE A JEW, LIVE LIKE A GENTILE AND NOT LIKE
A JEW, WHY ARE YOU FORCING THE GENTILES TO
TAKE UP THE JEWISH WAY OF LIFE?

Commentary

Cephas, by his hypocrisy, turning back to the norms of
law in a spirit of guilt, was teaching the Gentiles, too, a
false doctrine about the Christian message and the Christian way of life. Paul says he was "forcing the Gentiles to
take up the Jewish way of life." For, if Cephas was a
leader in the church, his example would be followed by
many. It would be presumed he had better knowledge
and good reasons for what he did. By the very act of
separating himself (and those who followed his example)
from the Gentiles, he was leaving them no choice. They
had to live separated from him (and the other Jews) or, if
they wanted to continue associating with them, they
would have to subject themselves to the Law completely.
But all Christians, all good Christians, would want to
associate with one another. Thus, if the Gentiles were

73

to be loving brethren, living in happy community and peace, they would have to live by the observance of the Law. This does add up to forcing them to "judaize"— that is, to take up the practice of the Law, as if the way of law were still the way for men to reach God. But Christian faith had liberated them from law and opened up a new way to please God, leaving men free for doing whatever love and loving sacrifice would call them to.

Thus there was, in Peter's action, a threat to the truth of the word of God. In the face of this threat, Paul speaks out. Lovers of good order might be horrified at his technique. He speaks out in front of all. He seems to show no concern for the possible scandal that simple souls might take. He shows no worry about covering up the mistakes of the leaders of the church. He does not help Cephas save face, explain himself, interpret his past or present actions. He does not help Cephas and the emissaries from James work out some compromise. He does not say: "Unity is our main concern; the organization must be protected. We can explain and justify what Cephas has done (for example, being 'a Jew to the Jews, a Greek to the Greeks'—1 Corinthians 10, 20f.)." He does not say: "If we give people the impression that their superiors and teachers cannot be trusted in such an important matter, they will not believe them in anything." He does not worry about the charge some will surely make: "This means anarchy! One cannot have people in the church, even great leaders like Paul, simply rising up and saying things without evidence. What text of the scriptures does he appeal to? What word of the Lord does he quote? What remembered tradition does he possess, that he should set himself against an apostle who lived with Christ personally when he walked the earth?" He makes no allowance for gradualism. He speaks out in front of all—and stands against Cephas, to his very face.

We reflected above that the Paul who wrote Galatians probably never thought of the Christian believers around the world as members of one all-embracing organization, and consequently would hardly have stopped to ask himself who was head of that organization. What he obviously did advert to was that there were recognized leaders of some kind in the church at Jerusalem—"those who seemed to be something" (Galatians 2, 2.6.7), "those who seemed to be pillars" (2, 9). There were those in Jerusalem who "were apostles before me" (1, 7).

Granting then at least that much priority to them, and considering the position of the Jerusalem church among the other churches, how would Paul's conduct and his own report on it here indicate he thinks eminent people in the church should be treated? The simplest expression of his rule would seem to be: they are to be supported and imitated when they are right; they are to be opposed and resisted when they are wrong. And who is to judge whether they are right or wrong according to the gospel? When it is a question of *my* reaction, *my* support and imitation versus my possible opposition and resistance, there is only one person who can make the final judgment. A sincere judgment of faith is called for, according to the norm of the greater love, practiced as sincerely as possible. In regard to my action, no one else but me can make that judgment.

It may be hard to speak up against one who holds a position of great respect. This must have been so for Paul here. Even though the Jerusalem church was hardly claiming a "primacy of jurisdiction," still, if people

75

around the world were beginning to look at it as the one especially well informed and especially safe to follow, any man would have to be careful in contradicting it.

This would be doubly true where the position to be opposed is one of the greater apparent piety. And such is the case here: the Jerusalem church was defending the apparently stricter and more holy position. It called for the way of life not only more conformable to tradition, but also more removed from ordinary, normal living, more "non-secular," and so, by an ever-popular false definition of the word, more "holy." It said: give up this and that food; practice this and that external observance; do not yield to your natural impulses of generous association. Submit, conform your judgment to that of the lawmaker, who holds the place of God. This Jerusalem approach would have a great appeal among people who were seeking only the greater and purer love and service of God. The loving, generous, pious soul would almost by instinct see it as the way more certainly pleasing to God simply because it was harder and more repugnant to nature. This is a perennial phenomenon of religious psychology. Paul would in contrast sound like a comparative libertine (as he was elsewhere and otherwise accused of being).

The whole situation would make it all the harder for him personally to stick to what he was sure was right. He may have known that the way of life he preached was a thousand times harder if put into practice. He also knew it was much less likely ever to be put into practice if people's attention came to be focused on a certain number of set external sacrificial observances which could themselves superficially calm and satisfy religious instincts. (Priests who preached abstaining from meat on Friday and fasting during Lent didn't use to be stoned in the street, as priests have been in our time for preaching interracial love. Which preaching did Catholic audiences find existentially harder?)

How did Paul then think a leader of the church should be treated? He seems to have agreed such a leader should be visited, informed, consulted, probably listened to. If the leader is accepted as leader, he is accepted as a sign of unity, and there should be signs of union with him. He should be spoken of respectfully, and it should be clear that one does not stand in flagrant opposition to him as to the essential nature of Christianity. We used above the phrase from later theology: "being in communion with" another church or head of another church. This phrase too could describe the relation a member of the church should have with a leader of the church. He should remain in communion with him and with the rest of the community through him.

The Christian leader has no authority of his own. His authority consists in two things: his mission to preach the gospel and his being able, as center of communion, to give expression to the common will of all those who are in communion with him. Insofar as he would ever command anything which was not (1) the pure preaching of the gospel, or (2) the general wish of his community (explicit or implicit, directly channelled to him or indirectly and representatively), such a statement of command would have no Christian effect on his "subjects" whatsoever. They might indeed obey out of fear—financial fear, superstitious fear, ambitious fear, or craven fear—but their obedience would not be an expression of their Christianity but of their cowardice.

One major consideration would seem to be lacking in our analysis of the church-order implicit in Paul's text.

That is, after all that has been said about independence, personal responsibility, judgment, what really remains for any personal "head of the church" to be or do? What would be the point of a personal headship, whether locally or universally anyway? Whether Paul explicitly thought about the possibility or not, what would it mean to have a recognized "head of the church" according to Pauline thought as shown in the texts we have considered? What could such a person be or do without conflicting with Pauline principles of Christian life?

We have ruled out giving orders which must be obeyed unquestioningly as from God. We have ruled out speaking the decisive and compelling word to other men on what is God's specific will for them in their individual circumstances. We have ruled out initiating all activity in the church. We have ruled out giving dispensations and such. We have ruled out making legalistic decisions except in cases where the law itself stems from him. (And, in the light of all Paul says here, how would it be thinkable that any Christian would ever be tempted to make laws for other Christians, at least any kind which would need special privileges and dispensations before the others would be free to serve God and live before him as they sincerely judge right?) What would a personal head of a church or of the universal church do, if he were not to arrange everyone's life for him? If Pauline liberty and self-determination should ever come to prevail among Christians, would there be any room at all left for personal headship in the church?

I think there still would, and that, as the membership of the churches grew and grew, extending into many lands, Paul himself might have been forced to recognize the legitimacy of such a role for someone, even if he may not have recognized it back then in regard to Peter. What might such a role be, remaining faithful to the Pauline judgments on all human authority and power, true to Pauline freedom for every Christian? Can we specify some of its positive characteristics?

We have indicated a first one above in considering Paul's initial visit to Jerusalem to see Cephas. Cephas was there. He was present, to listen to the account of what was happening in other churches. Presumably Paul knew he was there all the time, and so did other Christians. One did not need permission before acting, but one expressed or could express one's unity with him and with all believing brethren through him by letting him know what things God was working in you and others through his Spirit in you. And Peter heard and perhaps discussed it with you.

To put it another way, a central figure, with whom all are to remain in communion, might have the role of making communion easy. He would be there. He would be present for service. He could be a central office for information and communication of the churches with one another. If you told him what God was working through you in the East, he could tell you what was happening in the West and the North and the South as well. This information might modify your own judgments and plans. To hear all the works of the churches discussed in one center (or, in an age of print, television, etc., in and through one central organ of communication) would bring them all into a certain perspective which would be unattainable by one alone, concerned perhaps primarily, even exclusively, with his own area.

He would make communion easy also by his own practice of Christianity. Ideally, he would be an outstanding embodiment of the Christian message in the world. By his love and suffering and willingness to sacrifice all for those who most needed help, he could be most perfectly the true vicar (replacement, representative, place-taker) of Christ in this world. By this he would indeed "having been himself converted, confirm his brethren" (Luke 22, 32). In that sense, one which the whole world could see and understand, he could truly be the Rock on which Christ's (universal) church stands built (Matthew 16, 18).

Next, (a further manifestation of how he might commend himself and Christ's love, making communion easy with him, and through him with all men) he would be an outstanding Christian pastor. That is, he would be himself an outstanding preacher and teacher of Christianity. (For this, supposing Rome continues as center of the Catholic church, he would naturally be an Italian. He would normally be a Roman. How else be a real preacher and teacher to the church at Rome?) He would preach the gospel, often and vividly and directly, by word and by example.

His style of life and the whole setting in which he lived would befit a successor of Peter the fisherman and a representative of the poor Christ. There would be nothing about him which could recall the princes and powers of this world or which would give the faintest support to suspicions that he or those around him dreamed of worldly power (crowns, thrones, military guards, palaces), put great store in worldly vanities (precious cloths, golden vessels, splendid jewels). "You know that those who are supposed to rule over the Gentiles lord it over them, and their great men exercise authority over them. But it shall not be so among you; but whoever would be great among you must be your servant, and whoever would be first among you must be slave of all" (Mark, 10, 42–44).

Such a center and head would be a great preacher and practicer of the gospel, the pure gospel. He might often fail in it; but it is still this that the community would look for from him. Better expressed, he would make the preaching of the gospel his main concern. He might be inadequate for it himself, but he would facilitate as much as possible and in every way possible the preaching mission of others. He would encourage the manifestations of the truth of the gospel and the power of the gospel wherever they might appear. And then, reciprocally, those who saw a value in so building up "one" church of Christ, that is, one recognizable external organization under that name, would always present the gospel in the world somehow in union with this man and in his name. They would then point to him as one whom all Christians should treat with respect and love because he was letting himself be used by the rest of the church and the churches as holding the place of Christ, as head and center and foundation stone and shepherd and servant. Rome would be a place to which Christians would travel to meet other Christians from around the world and share with them and hear from them the many-splendored works of the one Spirit.

This would be one way of "feeding Christ's lambs and sheep" (John 21, 15–17). Another would be that all men would know appeals for help in need could always be directed to and through this one center or head. This would be especially true when an individual Christian community or a large group of communities was in serious difficulty. When, for instance, the work they had undertaken was clearly beyond their powers, they would call

81

for help from other Christian churches, and normally, naturally, they would channel their call of distress through the center of the church.

Again, he would be the natural one to direct the attention of the various parts to the needs of other parts or to the needs of the whole. It would be his task in a special way to keep turning the eyes of men in one part of the world to unfinished tasks for the Christian in other places. Encyclicals like "On the Progress of Nations," concerned with the welfare of those most easily overlooked (in this case, many of those non-Christian peoples) would seem very much one of his proper concerns and projects. The (rumored but still unpublished) encyclical on "Interracial Justice and Love" might be another. Similarly, the push towards peace, reminding Christian men everywhere of the wider and truer perspective in which men killing men is folly and never a solution to the problems of the world, would seem to be the kind of thing a head of the church might exist to do.

Even prayer and sacramental life could well be his concern, showing or rather helping the rest of the churches to see in the contemporary world how to make their gatherings in Christ's name more meaningful, more expressive of their faith and their dedication. He could do this and would be expected to, even if the Pauline point of view would not leave much room for his deciding what exact rubrics to follow or language to use. People would look to him for a stimulus to love and service on the widest possible front, even though they no longer in any way felt bound to ask him whether they could or could not marry, have children, give expression to personal love. If he did write on birth control or sacerdotal celibacy, he would probably be read simply as one well-informed and concerned Christian giving his personal opinion, because intimate, personal vocations and decisions are so much a part of these. But if he wrote on the needs of the world of his day, especially insofar as they crossed diocesan and national boundaries, he would be looked to as a sign, an expression of the aspirations of Christianity in the world, spokesman for all believers, insofar as they together were "the gathering," the one church." This too would be a way of feeding the flock entrusted to his care (1 Peter 5, 2). It would also be his way of seeing fulfilled the promise "Whatever you bind on earth will be bound also in heaven" (Matthew 16, 19). For this promise, which was given in the same words to all the disciples in Matthew 18, 18, implies that the work of the pastors in the churches has heavenly, eternal effects. This would be especially true of the work of the chief pastor.

Thus, considering his recognized central position, he would be responsible in a special way for helping the church as a whole to choose the particular directions in which it wanted to move from age to age. It would be his special responsibility to look at the whole world situation and suggest: "Here are today's special needs. I think the attention of all Christians ought to be directed in a special way to the following outstanding needs of our time. Here is where a Christian service of love and sacrifice is especially needed today."

Another function of him who would be head of the church would take the form of passing judgment on charisms. That is, the Spirit presumably works through the people of God. Reports would be made to a central headquarters, as explained earlier. His job would be first to listen and to be a center of exchange for ideas and inspirations. But more than that, his work would be the positive one of helping keep the church open to all possible manifestations of the Spirit. Consequently, there would be the need for judging in the name of the whole church that such and such a supposed manifestation of the Spirit is not after all useful—after it has been tested —*for the whole church as one universal church.* Note he does not decide whether or not it is useful or good *for you,* for this or that individual church. That is up to those on the spot to decide before God and their consciences. He, however, can be the organ the church uses or through whom all Christians freely choose to work in making decisions on the value of movements, charisms, activities, ideas, and inspirations which call for a reaction from *the whole church,* or claim to have a message or task for the church as a whole.

Even that judgment would not pretend infallibly to categorize the movement as right or wrong in itself. It would simply be a practical judgment as to whether it will receive the positive active support of the church group as a group here and now. Paul does this in various letters himself. It is part of the job of good order, and therefore of normal administration in any large group. But in the church of God it naturally bears on spiritual things. It need not involve excommunications or other measures of repression, for "if this plan or this undertaking is of men, it will fail, and if it is of God you will not be able to overthrow it" (Acts 6, 28f.).

Now in all these things, a man can fail. He can and sometimes will fail, just because he is a man. Cephas, for instance, in the example from which our reflections began, obviously was failing to fulfill the role of rallying point, symbol of unity, rock and foundation, confirmer of the faith. When such a man fails, the church can and should rebuke him. If he prove obstinate in his error, the church can and should replace him. For he is center and sign of unity and all the rest because the church has need of such. And if he is also a central organ for communication in the church and instrument for reaching decision on programs of action, and for stimulating the brethren to a universal viewpoint, it is because the church has need of these things and chooses to localize them in him. But she does so in order to realize better the gospel in practice. She does so as one way of living the gospel effectively in the real world. This monarchic organization has its advantages, and in history has worked about as successfully and as often in the church (politically considered) as it has in the civil area. But to unite so many different functions in one man is not a necessary expression of the gospel. Where it is adopted, as it has been by Roman Catholicism, it still must be practiced as a hegemony conformable to the gospel and constantly judged by the gospel. That is the kind of gospel leadership which we have tried to describe, taking the norms basically from Paul. The fact that the manner of practicing leadership in the Roman Catholic church has not actually conformed historically in all details to what has been described should not be allowed to confuse the issue. The issue is, a form of church order which would (1) have a single leader, as Cephas may have been in some respects the leader of the church in Paul's day; and (2) not violate the basic reality of Christian liberty which is so important to Paul. In other words, if Paul thought Peter was chief shepherd, how did he, how could he, live with the situation?

Now the Pauline criteria, as we have seen, are not

easily reconcilable with control from above, a chain of command, with tight hierarchical ordering and subordination. Paul simply did not recognize such things as Christian. His attitude toward them would be that they are human. And so they have in fact developed in the Catholic church—as human realities, not evil in themselves, but certainly not God-given, distinctively Christian, nor essential to the church in all ages. The church brought them in out of a felt need at certain times for good order, besides out of human desires for power and for preservation of property and wealth from generation to generation. Today, where the concern for power is surely not as great as it once was among churchmen, they seem necessary only to the extent that many in governing positions feel conscience-bound, out of loyalty to the institution, to preserve "the church's" wealth and power intact for those who will succeed them. But such thinking is wrong by Pauline norms and by gospel norms. Their conscience is bound without reason.

For as power, property and wealth are not the proper concerns of Christians as such, so they are not proper concerns of the church as such. Hence Christians need have no fear that what they feel called to do might undermine a structure which exists mainly to preserve and guarantee the continued preservation of things like these. God will still preserve the true church. They must begin to believe really that when a man fails or when all men or all human means fail, still the church cannot fail. Through it all, the church as such has been promised idefectibility. She will experience it, though her members may not. The Lord did not say to Peter: "The gates of hell will not prevail against *you.*" He said, "against *her.*"

The center of unity of the universal church then, could not have the function of giving orders and making laws and taking away individual responsibility and judgment and free decision. But he would be, in and through the functions we have described, a symbol and a rallying point for all who call themselves Christian. That is, whatever his personal abilities or lack of them, he would supply, simply by being there, something the church as a living community has need of. Christianity, as Paul's letter has made clear down to this point, is very much a matter of individual decision and the individual courage of faith. If it is also to express itself in a community, as Christian thinkers generally agree it should, then some further element is needed. Love and the desire to help others is not sufficient explanation of that added element, for Christians presumably want to love and help all others, not just those who are willing to form community with them. Again, faith alone is not a sufficient foundation or criterion of Christian community, for faith itself is invisible, and when it does work itself out in practice, it may do so in very diverse ways.

But through such a figure as we have described, believers might recognize one another in spite of the invisibility of their faith and love. They could recognize one another as in communion with him. Other forms and manifestations of essential unity could have been developed. But in fact they were not, until the Reformation. And even after the Reformation, this way of unity through communion with the one church and man remained standard for the vast majority of Christians. Even many of the Reformation churches retained the essentials of the system, to the extent that they retained episcopacy, where again the mark of unity in one church,

87

one local church, is continued communion with one man as bishop. It is again only one of perhaps hundreds of possible systems of ultimate decision making. This operation could equally well have been performed by diocesan, national and international councils and synods. Instead, it was done by the one man or his agents. It could be changed, however. Now that it exists, where it exists, we say here only that it must conform to the Pauline principles of self-determination, self-responsibility, and Christian freedom.

But all our reflection, we admit once again, is only implicit in this epistle. It is needed only because later Christians naturally ask and wonder what Paul would say about the church of those later ages. They wonder what he would say of the church in which it has been taken for granted that there is and must be such a thing as chief pastor of the church, and one principal church among the churches. When they read Paul's dealings with Cephas in the light of the actual shape the church has taken in history, they cannot help asking such questions as have been raised here. And that and that alone is the reason they are raised here. There is no intention of arguing that Paul actually looked on Cephas or anyone else as "head of the church." That cannot be demonstrated from this letter or from anything else Paul wrote. Nor is it to be found stated in the other writings of the New Testament.

Two final points. (1) Why did Paul not fear the danger of splitting the church by his action? For if Peter was the head, would not such a split have been a possible consequence of facing up to him? Or, perhaps more importantly, why would it not be a serious problem for the later church? The reason might be, first, that Christ promised the church would endure. Secondly, it might be that the church according to the Pauline notion and constructed in accord with his principles cannot be split. If the important thing in the church is the faith and love and commitment of the members, how can that be split? In any arguments, after the arguments, disputes, contradictions, the number of real believers remains the same. Some believe and live and are saved and some will never be.

That is what matters, not external details of tight organization. The external apparatus, structures, of the church can be split, yes. Some can say, "I agree with X" and some, "I agree with Y." This is evident from the first four chapters of 1 Corinthians. But even there, Paul's protests against what was going on were not protests over the fact that not all were saying the same thing, but over the fact that in the midst of their differences they were not loving one another and accepting one another. They were not living like Christians, for they were not understanding, forgiving, loving. They were fighting, disputing, forming factions to seek their own advantages.

But there would be no problem of unity, no danger of being split, for a church which rests heavily on faith and love expressed in the most complete openness in small group meetings, content with "communion" with other groups, desirous meanwhile to do good to all men. That danger could arise only when there was question of one group entering in and trying to disturb another, when they denied the validity of another's Christianity or commitment, when they took to interfering with one another, judging one another.

On the other hand, it could make not the slightest difference that the different groups, when meeting separately to express their Christianity, their own faith and love and sacrifice and service and commitment, did things differently and expressed things differently. It could not matter that different groups used different forms, rites, images, language, ceremonies, gestures; different theological approaches, different images, different philosophies, literatures, psychologies. That different groups decided, for Christian reasons, that they were bound to take different, even opposed courses of action, could do no harm to their unity in Christ in faith and love. How could it? Why should it? What greater unity is needed than the knowledge that elsewhere in this world there are other people as committed as oneself to a gospel as crazy as one's own—the proclamation that the crucified one is the Lord of glory? That death is life and suffering is joy—when love transforms them all?

Therefore, even if Cephas was indeed for the church of Paul's time the "center of unity" which the gospels later imply Peter did become, still there was no harm in someone's standing up to him. And there could easily be a duty to do so.

(2) If Paul speaks out so boldly and forcefully and with such concern over the question of legalism when it concerned obedience to that which he and his readers believed to be the very law of God, then one must wonder indeed what he would have said about returning to a pattern of legalism in regard to man-made laws—even if (or perhaps especially if) those laws were made by the men who hold positions of power in the church. Think, for example, how this story might have been told had Cephas's "hypocrisy" had to do with the observance of laws Cephas himself or the rest of the twelve had

made! Can Paul's dismay, anger, horror, even be imagined?

What would he have said had he been present when the first "laws of the church" were made? Not that he did not think, as any sane man must, that a community, if it is to act as a community, must have regulations. If they are, to take a simple example, going to meet for the eucharist, they must meet at some time in some place and follow some order in their proceedings. And someone or some method or some body or some laws must determine all this. That is merely human.

But that is the point: it is human. It is not man's means of contact with the divine. Obedience to it is not the direct way of finding and knowing and serving God's will. It is simply a practical necessity. Paul would not have objected on the day such "traffic regulations" were devised. But he would have objected violently on the day someone claimed that such laws were the manifestation of God's will to men; that one could sin by disobeying them; that one could and should seek sanctity by obeying them, by committing oneself to them; that one was less a Christian for ignoring them. If observance of the law of *God* has become for the Christian a thing of lesser value and comparative indifference, how much more must the observance of any law of any *man*.

With the way he sometimes has of urging tolerance on either side, (see especially Romans 14, 1–12), the very best Paul would say—supposing he did not attack violently—would probably be something like this: "Let ecclesiastical bureaucrats and politicians amuse themselves by making all those regulations if they really enjoy it. But don't *you* pay any attention to what they come

91

up with unless, of course, it is clearly something necessary or useful for the service of the community and the world. Don't you feel bound by them at all, just because the laws are there. Law in itself is nothing. And no law can be an expression of God's will taking precedence over your only law, the law of the love of Christ."

"Just go on living," he would probably say. "Go on being as good a Christian as you can. Do good in the world, letting your faith work through love. If they curse you, fulminate against you, excommunicate you, pay no attention. What harm does that do you? Live in love. Serve. Teach. Exhort. No man can ever stop you from this."

Text and Paraphrase

2, 15   WE ARE JEWS BY BIRTH, AND NOT SINNERS FROM AMONG THE GENTILES—sinners we are in any case (see Romans 3, 9ff.). But we—that is I, Paul and Cephas and some of you my readers—were born into a group where we inherited the idea that a man was good or bad, really good or bad in the eyes of God, according to whether he kept the Law or not. God had laid down certain laws and demanded their observance as a sign of fidelity to him, as a token of love for him and of general human submission to him. God had laid down good laws, beautiful laws, for the relation of man to man, of man to society, for the control of ritual worship, for the uplifting of everyday life and sanctifying of the most normal and often neglected aspects of human living. God demanded obedience. In some parts of our scriptures he demanded it for its own sake, simply because He was Lord and Master. In others he demanded obedience as a sign of fidelity and love. But in any case, he demanded complete and perfect obedience to his laws.

The greatest sign of love a man could show was to study God's laws day and night and endeavor to conform his life to them in every way. If we were true to the Law, we thought we would be rewarded. God had promised it again and again in the prophets. If we were untrue, even in the smallest detail, we would be punished. This is the tradition in which we were raised. We did not make it up of ourselves. Our sacred books were filled with this idea. This was our inheritance by birth into the Jewish people, and we looked on it as a wonderful privilege. "What other nation has had its gods so close to it?" God had manifested his will for the carrying out of life. What greater lot for men, what more sublime ideal, than to try to carry out that will in all its fullness? This was the good man—and the poor other nations, blinded, following each its own way, they were "sinners"—they did not live according to the divine will. Indeed, how could they possibly, not even knowing it?

2, 16   BUT KNOWING NOW THAT A MAN IS NOT MADE GOOD BY THE WORKS OF THE LAW EXCEPT INSOFAR AS HE HAS FAITH IN JESUS MESSIAH, WE TOO—Jews though we are—HAVE BELIEVED IN MESSIAH JESUS SO THAT this can happen to us too, so that WE MAY BECOME TRULY GOOD in the eyes of God THROUGH FAITH IN CHRIST AND NOT THROUGH WORKS OF LAW. BECAUSE the Law itself teaches us: FROM WORKS OF LAW NO ONE AT ALL WILL EVER BECOME WHAT HE SHOULD.

Yes, we have now, as Christians, passed far beyond our former state of mind. The laws are still there, but they are no longer to us the measure of the goodness of a man. A man is not good in the eyes of God because he keeps these laws. A man is good who pins his life on Christ and on faith in the cross of Christ as the way to salvation. This faith gives a man absolute norms of love and sacrifice and fidelity—norms so absolute that they will demand far more of a man than any collection of laws ever could; but also so absolute that they must be followed even where laws stand in the way; and finally norms so absolute that they make law pale into insignificance as a way to God. The way of faith is the direct way to God, and we have seen the light when we became Christians. We have chosen to follow that way.

In fact, our basic insight is that even for those who follow or who ever in the past followed the way of law, it was never really the simple fact of their observances which actually made them good in the eyes of God. Even those people of our nation, the heroes of the whole Old Testament, were *good* because they lived in faith and to the extent to which they lived in faith—a faith which, except for its *explicit* object, was identical with our faith today. It was faith in a God who made a world which is basically good and for our good, a God whom we love even though he slay us (Job 13, 15). It was faith that the world, as God's creation, was a thing of great value, worth working for and saving; faith that our fellow men are of such tremendous value we can rightly give our whole selves without limit to their service and love.

This attitude of mind and this direction given to one's life has always really been the measure of the goodness of a man before God. I can call it "faith in Jesus Messiah" even though many of the people who lived it died long before Jesus' birth. For the faith I have described was always faith in a Messiah; that is, in a redemption to come. It was faith that, no matter how unrewarding and frustrating life from day to day might seem, God would someday reward his people's suffering and patience by sending a chosen one to transform the world in joy. And the man, Jesus, whom all eyes have seen as the crucified one and whom our tongues have witnessed to as risen from the dead, this Jesus does sum up perfectly the elements of that perennial faith of Israel: how it is to be clung to even in the darkest moments of life and imminent death; held in the face of the greatest apparent perversions of right order and justice; how it cannot fail to climax in raptured resurrection. Our fathers never heard of Jesus of Nazareth, but they believed that Israel, though seemingly poor and weak and ever abused, remained the object of God's special predilection. They never ceased to believe that no matter how low she had fallen or been crushed, no matter how completely she seemed to have been abandoned, God would raise her soon to unimaginable heights of glory. This is the same faith which I preach today. It is fulfilled in Jesus of Nazareth, and to have it means a man is right before God and able to live in the world as God made him to live.

We know this now, it is part of our new Christian insight. Faith in Christ Jesus is what makes a man right, not fidelity to the works of law. Careful observance of laws may indeed have been a *sign* of the possession of this faith in the past. But the justification of a man even then came not from the works but from the faith.

And that is why we have now put our faith explicitly in Jesus as Messiah, in order that this may really and explicitly and openly happen to us. We don't even want to pretend we are seeking justification before God by works of law. We say openly, "No, our rightness before God is no more than our faith." Because after all it is the Law itself which teaches us "by works of law no man at all can be justified."

As a matter of fact, we learn this same truth not only from the Law's words. Experience has helped us here too. For just think: God has laid down his laws—have we ever really fulfilled them? Oh, we can fulfill the small externals well enough. We can offer a lamb each morning and one each evening. We can measure out the fine flour and sprinkle the oil and frankincense. We can wear the sacred clothes commanded, attend the right rituals, say the right prayers. If we are careful enough, we may occasionally do them all without one mistake. But what about: Love your neighbor as yourself? What about: Thou shall not covet? What about: Thou shalt not have strange gods before me? Have we really lived up to all that is demanded by commandments such as these? Have we ever kept all God's laws? And if we ever should do so, what about the moments of life for which no law provides? Measure ourselves sincerely according to what the law of God asks of us and none of us deserves to be called a good man.

2, 17   AND IF, AS WE SEEK TO FIND OUR GOODNESS IN CHRIST alone, WE HAVE BEEN FOUND by others TO BE not just and good but rather found to be OURSELVES SINNERS—WHAT THEN? Are we to admit that CHRIST IS AN AGENT OF SIN? CERTAINLY NOT!

Commentary

Here is another problem. It will arise as soon as someone tries to put the consequences of this doctrine into practice so we had better consider it at once. Cephas's fear in the face of the Jerusalem emissaries illustrates it perfectly. Suppose we have turned from attention to laws and put all our attention on living the gospel we have believed. Love and sacrifice become the standard of our choices. The unselfishness of the crucified becomes the norm for judging the right thing to do in every individual case. Failures there are, have been, and will be, but we throw them too on the cross of Christ—that is, we say before God, *that* is the life we accept, believe in, hope to live; that is the self-offering we want to express in our own lives. Where we fail, look not to our sins, Father; look to our faith, our desires, our intentions—look to the perfect act of loving self-giving which he once offered in your sight.

Suppose we make the gospel our principle, the cross our standard and our life. And then along come the legalists! "What is this?" they say to a priest. "You have shared the eucharist with heretics? You have failed to recite your Office? You have attempted marriage?" Or to a layman: "You have missed mass on Sunday? You want to divorce this woman? You are practicing birth control?" "But," we respond, "there was this child to be looked after. There was this friend to be consoled. There is this love to be preserved, this confidence not to be betrayed."

"But the Law?"

"The Law was not made for such things as this. The Law of itself is nothing. Faith which works through love is everything."

The legalists who came to Paul in the story he just related had accused him and Cephas of violating the Law by eating with unclean people; they had accused him, or were about to accuse him and Cephas, of violating laws of cleanliness. Indeed he had violated them. So had Cephas. Although being Jews, they had "lived as Gentiles and not as Jews" (v. 14). But God's law was clear—terribly clear.

The Jews had adhered to their law with love and loyalty in the face of terrible persecution. Now Paul and Cephas neglected it. Why? The reasons in this particular instance are not specified, but from the context, one reason would suffice. They ate with Gentiles because these Gentiles were their fellow Christians, and it is better to eat with people with whom one wants to be brotherly, friendly, than not to eat with them. The Law forbade it. But in this instance, that would mean the Law forbade love and friendship. But the faith in Christ's cross makes love an absolute norm, and so the prohibition of the Law here loses its meaning.

The Catholic of today tends to ask whether the same situation could have arisen as regards laws which were not merely ritual. Of course they could have, and of course they do. But first, it is not well even to make the distinction between ritual laws and others. They are all equally the law of God in the mind of the church Paul was raised in. If obedience was the norm, and God was the source of the law, then there could be no distinctions between law and law. All were equally holy and equally binding. And remember, many men went to

99

death for these laws towards which Paul was now—apparently—to his fellow Jews—acting so cavalierly.

But, to go ahead and make the distinction which seems so natural to us—could the same bind occur in regard to laws which were not merely ritual? Could it occur in regard to God's own ten commandments? Obviously. Sabbath violation is a clear case, with examples furnished by the gospel from our Lord's own life. But adultery? Yes, even adultery, stealing, murder. Of course, moralists have over the ages worked out refined definitions for stealing and murder which leave room for "exceptions"—that is, which make the exception "not really stealing or murder," for instance, in cases of need or of extreme personal danger. But in fact, in terms of the Law itself, such cases are exceptions to the Law. They are instances of "situation ethics" but situations which arise so frequently that they have, by an extended interpretation of the text, been incorporated into the laws themselves.

But there are plenty of other situations which have not been so worked into the standard general interpretations and redefinitions of the law, because they occur less frequently or because they vary too widely and too unpredictably. But they are no less true or less serious for that. Such situations may arise in any man's life, and some of them will arise in every man's life. When they arise, they call for a decision. And the decision will not be adequately made by the norms of law alone. As modern writers on situation ethics have often noted, the only reason we do not perceive such situations frequently in our own lives is that we habitually avoid facing independently and courageously the need to make a personal assessment of the world in which we live. We are content in general to do what everyone else does. And so we support tyrannies by our silence and profit from social structures which exploit the helpless and never feel personally the responsibility to reform or revolution.

But some men do perceive more deeply and are more courageously ready to take the responsibility of acting when they see a need. When we are among the number of such men, then the legalists rise up and say, "How can you do that? You're breaking the law!" Our answer is, "Justice, charity, self-sacrifice, truth, recognition of the here-and-now real-world situation demands that I do what I'm doing, at least insofar as I can judge the here-and-now situation. And these are the Christian norms of action summed up in the love of Christ. Sorry about the Law. This is bigger than the Law."

Then they are scandalized. Then they say "You are sinners." They may even turn away saying, "You talk of the Messiah, but your following him only leads you to sin. Your religion is only a pretext for sin. Or perhaps it is a cause of sin. We will stick with Moses and the laws. We know God spoke to Moses, but as to this Christ of yours, we know not from where he is" (see John 9, 29).

So there we are, labelled sinners, for trying to do what we thought right. Now the label is clearly deserved, according to the norms of *law*. Only those are not our norms. To *them*, then, Christ is "an agent of sin." Our allegiance to the norm of faith in him has made us "sinners." Are we to admit this? Not in any real sense. It is true only according to their norms, not according to ours. Are their norms better? They are clearer. They are more exactly expressed. One can know whether oneself

101

or another person has observed a certain law. One can never know about another whether he has acted out of pure love; nor even be all that sure about oneself.

The Law says you may not eat this food. The Law says you may not marry this woman. Paul says, too bad. Love is the norm. And that norm says, as far as I can tell, go ahead and do it. The legalists will call the followers of Paul men who teach abominations in foods and fornication (Revelation 2, 10). Too bad. They called Jesus a wine-bibber and a glutton (Luke 7, 34).

But is not their norm better in the sense of being objective—that is, that they "know God spoke to Moses?" Well, hardly. This will take another long discussion and is perhaps best left for another time and place to discuss, but in brief: their "knowledge" that God spoke to Moses is after all only their faith judgment in the divine origin of the Law. It is no more and no less "objective" than our faith judgment that a new and absolute norm has been given us in Christ. Who knows when a man opens his mouth whether that man speaks in the place of God or not? Many men have claimed this for themselves. No man can ever "prove" it. Ultimately, it is always the individual believer and the individual believing community on whom responsibility must fall for judging whether the word spoken is indeed the word of God or not.

It is not Christ who makes me a sinner nor is it following the norms of Christ and of faith which declares me a sinner. The legalists consider me a sinner because they hold to the norms of the laws alone. I have transcended those norms to rise to the norms of faith and love alone. I am a sinner only if I return to those other norms. Then I have indeed transgressed the law. So let me not say that when legalists find me and judge me a sinner, then Christ is to go down as an agent of sin. Be-

2, 18   cause the reality is simply this: IF I SET BACK UP THE NORMS WHICH I HAVE rejected and DESTROYED FOR MYSELF, THEN I, not Christ, MAKE MYSELF A TRANSGRESSOR. If in fear I return to the norm of law, then I must return as a confessed sinner and transgressor.

2, 19   But that is not my situation. FOR I HAVE DIED TO THE LAW—and as a matter of fact, I did so not out of disloyalty to the Law but out of the deepest, truest loyalty to the Law. Belief in the Law as word of God has led me to reject finally the Law and the way of law as norm of my life. The Law itself has taught me that there is no being justified before God by observance of the Law. Before God we remain terrible sinners, we continue to fail in observance of the Law just as we always have. The Law itself teaches me that true justice is the justice, the goodness, of faith. I'll demonstrate this later (3, 7). Moreover, the Law itself teaches me, as I'll explain in a moment (3, 13), that Christ Jesus, in the death he suffered, was an object of God's curse and rejection. But that is absurd and the flat contradiction of my faith that Jesus is Christ and Lord. Therefore, the Law itself leads me, if I am at the same time to believe in Christ, to something beyond itself, to a judgment I cannot help making. The Law itself leads me to conclude that its own worst curses are something not to be feared, but rather to be transcended, boldly faced and even embraced, when love demands it. I have then, as I say, died to the Law as norm of my life, and I did so out of the Law itself, out of my very real faith in it and love for it. I did SO IN ORDER THAT I MIGHT TRULY LIVE TO GOD. I stand condemned by this Law but I stand condemned with Christ. And I accept the Law's punishment with Christ. WITH CHRIST I AM NAILED TO THE CROSS.

2, 20   AND NOW, I LIVE NOT I, BUT THERE LIVES IN ME CHRIST. WHAT I NOW LIVE HERE IN THIS FLESH I LIVE IN FAITH, my faith IN GOD'S OWN SON WHO LOVED ME AND DELIVERED HIMSELF even to the curse of the Law FOR ME, that I might know the truth of things and adjust my life accordingly.

2, 21   I AM NOT GOING TO SET ASIDE THE GIFT GOD HAS GIVEN ME. It is too tremendous. But that's what you are asking me to do if you ask me to return to the norm of law. BECAUSE IF MAN'S RIGHTNESS and goodness IS TRULY FROM OBSERVANCE OF LAW THEN CHRIST MIGHT JUST AS WELL NOT HAVE DIED AT ALL.

His death was useless if it was not the communication to us who believe in him of an altogether new principle of operation, quite apart from any norm of law.

3, 1 YOU FOOLISH GALATIANS, WHO HAS BEWITCHED YOU THEN? YOU ARE THE MEN BEFORE WHOSE EYES JESUS CHRIST WAS PAINTED CLEARLY—AND IT WAS CHRIST THE CRUCIFIED!

I was with you not so long ago. I told you of Christ and his disgraceful death. I preached to you the unbelievable message that called for your utter belief and devotion. I told you that the man who was nailed to the cross was the Messiah, the Savior, the Lord of Glory. I portrayed him to you, the crucified failure, object of rejection of God and of man, and I said: "Here is your way of salvation: self-giving even to that point. Here is your law: love unto death. Here is the good man—the one who can believe in the God who gives you this as your picture of salvation, hope, life, joy, reward. Can you believe it? Then you are one of God's chosen ones and the future belongs to you. Can you believe it? Can you undertake to live by it, even when the upholders of law as the pattern of life threaten you with the same punishment they finally visited on him? Can you? Will you?"

You heard and you believed. Christ crucified was your life. Well, what has happened to you now? How can you be turning to another norm, the old norm of law?

3, 2 LET ME ASK YOU THIS, DID YOU RECEIVE THE SPIRIT

FROM WORKS OF LAW OR FROM HEARING AND BE-
LIEVING? ARE YOU SO MINDLESS THEN? YOU MADE
YOUR BEGINNING IN SPIRIT AND NOW YOU WANT TO
END UP IN FLESH. HAVE YOU SUFFERED SO MUCH THEN,
ALL IN VAIN (IF IT WAS REALLY SO POINTLESS . . .)?
THE ONE WHO GAVE YOU THE SPIRIT AND WORKED
POWERS IN YOUR MIDST, DID HE DO IT FROM WORKS
OF LAW OR FROM HEARING AND FAITH?

3, 3

3, 4

3, 5

You, most of you, were not raised in the Jewish
community as I was. You never heard in your
youth of the Law I knew. But take it or take
your own civil law if you like; it makes no difference. You received the spirit of Christ when you
became a Christian. There entered your life an
experienced change, a difference you have known,
felt, can and do tell others about. How did this
happen to you? Was it because you had observed
the Jewish laws? You never heard of them. Was it
because you had lived by your own laws? Nonsense.
Why had it never happened to you earlier?

No, dear children, the difference in your lives
now from what it was then, the difference so distinctive of you as Christians, came when you heard
the good news and believed it. Isn't that so? Isn't
that the moment when you began to feel God's
spirit active in your lives? Well then? What makes
you look for something else now? Who's been getting at you? Isn't the spirit enough for you then?
Do you want something more tangible? Nice material observances? Flesh?

You foolish Galatians. Faith is what is important. Hearing and believing. These have saved you
so far. They have made you good Christians up to

the present. Anyway, as I suggested above, one can find in the teaching of the Law itself that faith is the only way of salvation even for the people of Israel to whom the law of God once was given. Yes, this is taught in the Law itself. Do you doubt it? I'll prove it:

3, 6   THAT IS WHAT IS WRITTEN AFTER ALL, about Abraham himself.

Commentary

Here Paul moves into another subject that hardly has immediate resonances for the modern reader. He starts to talk about Abraham and to worry about who are the true sons and heirs of Abraham. He worries about God's covenant and God's promises made, supposedly, many hundreds of years before his own time. And he tries to explain, in terms of his own teaching about faith and life, what those promises must really have meant.

At this point Paul is simply in the position of any great religious thinker. He must account for the past tradition of the faith-community to which he belongs. Paul thought of himself as a Jew with a new insight into what Judaism really meant. A new understanding of life and the world and the God-man relationship had come to him through his hearing of Jesus. But he saw this new understanding as completely coherent with all that was best in his own previous faith-tradition. He saw it in fact as the fulfillment of all the good things which he had perceived and felt imperfectly in his own Jewish faith before.

But that means he had to be able, as a theologian, to

explain himself and his insight in terms of that older faith-tradition. He had grown up in a faith-community which believed that God had broken into human history about eighteen hundred years previously with a special revelation of himself to a man named Abraham. The revelation had also involved a promise to bless Abraham and his descendants and to give them the land of Israel for their secure possession forever.

That same faith-tradition believed that Abraham and one certain line of his descendants had responded to God's revelation and lived in hope in God's promise and in loyalty to the God who had revealed himself. This line was the one that ran through Isaac and Jacob and Jacob's twelve legal sons.

When Joseph, one of these twelve sons, after a series of adventures, finally came to a position of power in the land of Egypt, the whole family went to join him there. There, over a period of some four hundred years, faith-tradition told that the family expanded to six hundred thousand members—in fact, an entire nation. But it also fell out of favor with the rulers of Egypt and, in the time of Moses—some thirteen hundred years before Paul, found itself in a state of slavery doing menial work for the Egyptians.

Moses gave the people new birth, leading them to freedom, out of Egypt, through the desert, and to the land which had been promised to Abraham. Paul's faith-community taught and believed that God had made a covenant, an agreement with the people under Moses, and given them a great collection of laws. If they kept the laws they were to be blessed with all prosperity. If they did not, they would be oppressed by enemies, they would suffer and even might temporarily lose the land which God had given them.

We have already considered the question of the sacredness of the laws above. We saw there the necessity Paul was under of justifying his teaching as we saw how scandalous that teaching must have seemed to people brought up in the thought of observance of law as the most perfect fulfillment of the will of God. This theme, Paul's defense and explanation, runs through the entire epistle. But in the verses that follow now, we will see Paul wrestling simultaneously with another concept fixed in the older faith-tradition: the concept of election. This was the idea, very much a part of the faith of Israel, that God had chosen them and had promised something special to *them*, to Abraham and to his descendants. God's promise of special favor was to the children of Abraham, not to the other nations. And so it is important for Paul to show the connection of what he preaches with the old traditions in regard to Abraham. It is important to examine the promises made to Abraham and the law given to Moses and to discuss the question of whom each one is for, under what conditions each was given, and what each was supposed to achieve. Without all this, there could be no integration of Paul's message about God's plan for men's salvation with the older traditions of the faith community which Paul himself believed to be genuine, holy, true and good.

Faith was for Abraham too the only way of salvation. His believing God's word is what made Abraham worthy of the name of good. "ABRAHAM BELIEVED GOD, AND IT WAS COUNTED FOR HIM AS GOODNESS." YOU CAN SEE FOR YOURSELVES, from that very statement of the Law itself: THOSE WHO LIVE BY FAITH and hope for justification by faith and count their goodness only to the extent that they have faith in God's word in Christ, THEY and they alone ARE really ABRAHAM'S SONS.

3, 7

3, 8 FOR SCRIPTURE ITSELF (that is, the Author of scripture) KNEW VERY WELL WHAT WAS GOING TO HAPPEN. GOD knew his own plan for the future. He knew he WAS GOING TO MAKE THE NATIONS JUST, all of them, not only Israel, and he knew he was going to do it BY FAITH. AND KNOWING IT, he COULD and did GIVE THE GOOD NEWS OF IT TO ABRAHAM AHEAD OF TIME. It's right there in the Book of Genesis: "ALL NATIONS WILL BE BLESSED IN YOU." That's what he said to Abraham: all nations—SO THAT THOSE WHO ARE MEN OF BELIEF WILL BE BLESSED WITH THE BELIEVING ABRAHAM.

3, 9

Who did you think would be blessed? Those who live under the Law? Not according to that promise they won't. It says "All nations." All nations don't and won't live under the Law and yet God's state-

3, 10 ment makes a universal promise of *blessing*. NOW law doesn't make any universal promise of blessing. Quite the contrary. The Law very much sets up a universal threat of a curse, not a blessing. And THOSE WHO SUBSCRIBE TO THE Law and want to live from WORKS OF THE LAW LIVE UNDER that threat of CURSE. HERE IS WHAT THE LAW SAYS: "CURSED IS HE WHO DOES NOT ABIDE BY ALL THE THINGS WHICH ARE WRITTEN IN THIS BOOK OF THE LAW AND DOES NOT DO THEM."

3, 11 NO ONE CAN BE FOUND JUST BEFORE GOD BY FOL-LOWING THE WAY OF LAW. IT'S OBVIOUS. THE SCRIP-

3, 12 TURE SAYS: "THE JUST MAN LIVES BY FAITH." NOW that isn't the way the Law says a man will live, is it? Oh, no! THE LAW DOES NOT WORK FROM FAITH. THE LAW SAYS "HE WHO DOES THESE THINGS WILL LIVE BY THEM." That's quite a different story. Not faith but *practice*, achievement, that's what counts if you take the way of law. And you are bound to achieve "every one of these things written in the Law." But that's impossible. How then did we ever escape the fear of the curse which the Law holds over all our heads? (This is true of all us Christians, Jews first, but then you Gentiles too, now that you've heard of the Law and begun to worry about it.) How are we delivered from that

3, 13 curse and the fear of it? I'll tell you how. CHRIST DELIVERED US FROM THE LAW'S CURSE. How so? He simply walked freely into the middle of it. HE BECAME FOR OUR SAKE A cursed thing and an ob-ject of CURSE. He did—according to the letter of the Law itself and according to all those who hold

111

by the Law—FOR IT IS WRITTEN: "CURSED IS EVERYONE WHO IS HANGED FROM WOOD." Christ let that happen to himself. He did it for us. No one can now believe in him as God's chosen and God's son and our savior, the Lord of Glory, and at the same time continue to think that the observance of the Law and the avoiding of its curses is an absolute. Now love and sacrifice are the only absolute. He presented us with the message of love and sacrifice practiced even in defiance of what the Law says

3, 14 and threatens. So that's how it was achieved THAT THE BLESSING OF ABRAHAM COMES FINALLY TO THE GENTILES IN THE MESSIAH, IN JESUS. That's how it was achieved THAT WE MIGHT RECEIVE THE PROMISE OF THE SPIRIT THROUGH FAITH.

3, 15 Let's look at it another way. I WILL TAKE AN EXAMPLE FROM HUMAN LIFE, shall I, BROTHERS? Well then, let us take A MAN's promise, made in solemn form. Let's say he makes his LAST WILL AND TESTAMENT. It is SIGNED AND SEALED. Now NO ONE comes along when it is all signed and sealed that way and simply SETS it ASIDE. No one just throws it away OR PUTS ANOTHER IN ITS PLACE.

3, 16 WELL, that's what we have in the case of God and Abraham: a promise, signed and sealed. A testament; and THE PROMISES ARE SOLEMNLY AFFIRMED to belong "TO ABRAHAM AND TO HIS SEED." Now notice IT DOESN'T SAY "AND TO HIS SEEDS", that is, "and to his descendants," PLURAL. IT SAYS "TO HIS SEED," "his descendant." And that's SINGULAR. That seems to speak of *one*. "And to your seed." Well, we know who that one is. THAT ONE descendant IS CHRIST. That one is the Messiah.

3, 17   AND THIS IS MY POINT. WHEN THE LAW CAME ALONG FOUR HUNDRED AND THIRTY YEARS LATER, IT DID NOT INVALIDATE THAT SIGNED AND SEALED TESTA- MENT OF GOD. How could it? Even in human affairs that doesn't happen. The coming of the Law under Moses didn't cancel out what had been given ear- lier SO AS TO RENDER VALUELESS THE PROMISE that

3, 18   had been given to Abraham! It couldn't! But IF anyone should think that THE INHERITANCE COMES BY LAW to those only who observe the Law, then he would have to say that it did! THEN the in- heritance would NO LONGER come FROM a PROMISE. Then the Law took all meaning out of God's prom- ise. With the coming of the Law the promise no longer counted.

If the inheritance really comes to those who observe the Law by observing law, then you cannot say it comes according to God's promise to those who wait for it and believe that promise. One or the other! Take your choice! AND YET GOD GAVE the inheritance TO ABRAHAM AS A GIFT, a free gift, given freely to Abraham and to his seed, by and THROUGH God's PROMISE! Well, then! That's set- tled!

3, 19   SO WHAT ABOUT THE LAW, you ask? Doesn't it have any meaning or point at all? Why did God give a law if it was determined far ahead of time that the inheritance should come freely and as gracious gift as an exclusive result of promise? It would seem rather useless for God to have sent Moses and put the people through all the rigors of the Law for so long a time then, wouldn't it?

Well, that's another question. I'll tell you more

113

about the way I see it in a moment (3, 22–24; 4, 1–5). But for now, let's say this: THE LAW WAS ADDED ON to the promise already given. It was added on FOR THE SAKE OF TRANSGRESSIONS INDEED, but only temporarily. The Law was added on so people would have an idea of the way in which to walk, really as some direction spelling out the good life, guarding people against too many mistakes, pointing out general mistakes people might tend to make by nature. Moreover, by pointing out the inadequacies in the lives men were living, the Law might make them realize their own helplessness, reflect on it, and feel forced into a position of reliance on faith. Some of these things, I would guess, played their role in God's decision to give a law. But my main point is he wanted it to be temporary, an in-between, inadequate arrangement, to hold only UNTIL THE SEED, the descendant, CAME, the one TO WHOM THE INHERITANCE HAD BEEN PROMISED.

(The Law's lesser character incidentally is shown in the fact that it was really laid down by angels, not by God Himself. It was LAID DOWN BY ANGELS AND PASSED ON to men THROUGH A MEDIATOR, Moses. How do I know it was "laid down by angels?" Well, just think, if one person has to say something to a group, he can just say it, can't he? 3, 20 ONE PERSON DOESN'T NEED A MEDIATOR. You only *need* a mediator when a group wants to say something to a group. Group "A" talks to the mediator, Group "B" then listens to the mediator's summary of what they say, and it responds, also through the mediator. Well, here there was, in the case of the Sinai testament, a mediator, Moses. The people of God were group "B." Where was Group "A," that a mediator should be needed? GOD IS ONLY ONE, AFTER ALL. He's not a group. Understand? There must have been a group dealing with the people of God through Moses. Who else could that group be but the angels? I'll admit this Rabbinic exegesis can be mighty subtle at times. . . . But the promises to Abraham were made by God directly and personally.

3, 21   Well THEN, what am I implying, that THE LAW IS SOMEHOW CONTRARY TO THE PROMISES OF GOD? NO, NOT AT ALL. That would be a terrible thing to say. The Law is not contrary to the promises of God. It cannot be, FOR it too came from him. Oh, IF A LAW HAD BEEN GIVEN US WHICH REALLY WAS ABLE TO GIVE LIFE, as our opponents say God's law is now, then it would indeed be contrary to the promises. THEN MAN'S GOODNESS WOULD COME FROM his observance of LAW and not from his faith

3, 22   in the promises. BUT that is not the case. Instead, the real picture and the real function of the law that God did give us was something quite different. What was it? This: God in his HOLY SCRIPTURE LOCKED US ALL UP UNDER SIN, put rules about sin and the danger of sin and the possibility of sinning all around us, wrapped us up in these as in so many chains. That was what his revealed law did for us. Doesn't sound very nice, you say? Ah, but it was only done that way IN ORDER THAT THE PROMISE—which was always, remember, basically ROOTED IN FAITH IN JESUS AS MESSIAH—that the promise MIGHT actually BE GIVEN TO THOSE WHO

BELIEVED. The Law is not against the promises (see above v. 21) for it does not replace them. It prepares for the actual conferring of what was promised. All closed in by threats and dangers of sin, men would and did focus their attention beyond this world on the God who commanded, who directed their lives in faith in him and belief that he would give what he had promised if they were faithful to him and to his laws. Here was something, these laws, something concrete through which they could express their faith. Here was a day by day link with him who was otherwise totally beyond them. A life of faith then became for them precisely a life of keeping the law as well as possible. The law of Moses was, moreover, as adequate a fixed expression as possible of many of the typical patterns of the good human life.

But the Mosaic Law, even as every other law which has ever been invented, was not the perfect expression of the good life, nor was it the perfect expression of faith. Christ and his cross were that,

3, 23 and they alone. And SO BEFORE perfect FAITH DID COME, WE WERE HEDGED ROUND, locked in under,

3, 25 BOUND ROUND WITH THE LAW, always IN EXPECTATION OF THE FAITH THAT WAS GOING TO BE REVEALED. THAT MEANS THE LAW WAS like OUR TUTOR, leading

3, 24 us along the way TO CHRIST, THAT WE MIGHT BECOME TRULY GOOD BY FAITH. BUT NOW THAT perfect FAITH HAS COME, WE ARE NO LONGER UNDER that TUTOR.

But, back to our story of Abraham and the solemnly promised inheritance. We said (3, 7ff.) that all who believed were really sons of Abraham and so shared the inheritance promised him. We showed that those who chose the way of faith must have been the ones God promised would be blessed in Abraham (3, 9–14). Then we started to say that the promise was to Abraham and to his (singular) descendant (3, 16ff.), and that was going to be another argument that you were on your way towards all you need hope for as long as you clung to faith: you didn't need the Law. Remember? Shall we go on to finish the argument? It is for your good and to establish your freedom.

3, 26   All right then. YOU ARE ALL, you know, not only sons of Abraham through faith like his, but, THROUGH YOUR FAITH IN CHRIST JESUS, you are SONS

3, 27   OF GOD. FOR ALL OF YOU WHO WERE BAPTIZED IN CHRIST HAVE PUT CHRIST ON—that is what baptism is all about. You made Christ's life-thrust yours too. And that means you chose to be all that he is. The real you became what Christ is—and Christ is Son of God.

3, 28   In Christ THERE IS NO JEW OR GREEK, THERE IS NO SLAVE OR FREE MAN, THERE IS NO MALE OR FE-MALE. FOR YOU ARE ALL ONE IN CHRIST JESUS, and

3, 29   by your faith in him. Well then, IF YOU ARE CHRIST'S, YOU ARE THE SEED OF ABRAHAM, the descendant of whom God spoke. You are, in him, THE ONES WHO WILL INHERIT ACCORDING TO THE PROMISE.

I can carry this little parable on further if you like, and use it also to explain that business of being shut up under sin and under law so that the Law was like our tutor till Christ came and faith

4, 1   came. Shall I? WELL THEN: you mustn't be too surprised that men who were sons of Abraham, heirs

117

according to the promise, had a time of servitude to undergo, servitude to law. For AS LONG AS A HUMAN HEIR IS STILL A CHILD, HE DOESN'T REALLY DIFFER much in act and in living FROM just A SLAVE in the same house—really he doesn't. He's all bound round with rules and regulations that others have made for him and continue to make. And this is SO EVEN THOUGH HE IS in fact the OWNER OF THE WHOLE PLACE. The inheritance is

4, 2 his, but he can't do anything about it. HE IS UNDER GUARDIANS AND MANAGERS UNTIL THE TIME SET BY

4, 3 HIS FATHER. WELL, WE TOO, WHEN WE WERE CHILDREN and as long as we were children, were held down as servants, we DID OUR STRETCH OF SERVITUDE ALL CONCERNED WITH MATERIAL THINGS, the concrete regulations about the things OF THIS WORLD. We didn't get to pass judgment on them; they passed judgment on us. Laws about what to do and how to do it controlled our material existence in this world, and we were bound to them like so many slaves. In fact, we served them, you might say, rather than they us.

4, 4   BUT WHEN THE FULLNESS OF TIME CAME, GOD SENT HIS SON, MADE OF A WOMAN AND MADE UNDER

4, 5 THE LAW IN ORDER THAT HE MIGHT FREE THOSE WHO WERE UNDER LAW—that is, SO THAT WE COULD RECEIVE IN FACT THE POSITION OF SONS by our faith in him.

    Moreover, to turn now to you non-Jews, it is a

4, 6 proof THAT YOU ARE SONS too, (see 3, 2.4) that GOD HAS SENT THE SPIRIT OF HIS SON INTO OUR HEARTS CRYING "ABBA, FATHER." He has, hasn't he?

4, 7 This is your experience, isn't it? WELL THEN, YOU

118

ARE NO LONGER SLAVE in any sense either. YOU ARE A SON. AND you are AN HEIR THROUGH GOD. And all of this, without the slightest reference to your observance of law. It is all only a question of faith in Jesus as Christ.

Your stage of servitude as Gentiles was of course not the same as the preparatory stage of us Jews. But it was a servitude too, wasn't it? What did you do before Christ came to you through our

4, 8 preaching? AT THAT TIME YOU, NOT KNOWING GOD, WERE trapped IN your own kind of SLAVERY. You were slaves OF THOSE GODS WHICH WERE REALLY NO GODS at all. And my complaint to you, if you are now turning to the Jewish Law and desiring to bind yourselves with material observances and threats of punishment, my complaint to you is basically the same as mine to those who did know and follow the Law and now want to return to it or

4, 9 consider themselves bound by it: namely, NOW THAT YOU KNOW GOD (OR, BETTER, HAVE COME TO BE KNOWN BY GOD) HOW CAN YOU possibly TURN BACK TO THINGS SO WEAK AND POOR, mere tokens of reality, to material and external observances by law, —you know the ones I mean, THE ONES YOU NOW say you WANT TO LIVE UNDER AGAIN ONCE MORE?

4, 10 YOU START OBSERVING HOLY DAYS AND MONTHS AND

4, 11 TIMES AND SEASONS. I REALLY FEAR FOR YOU, THAT I MAY HAVE LABORED AMONG YOU IN VAIN. When you try to move from Christian faith to the external observances of the old religion, you are in practice taking up again essentially the same kind of servitude you knew as pagans.

4, 12 BECOME LIKE ME, BECAUSE I TOO AM LIKE YOU,

119

4, 13 BROTHERS. I BEG YOU. YOU HAVE IN NO WAY HARMED ME! YOU KNOW THAT ON ACCOUNT OF A WEAKNESS OF THE FLESH I CAME PREACHING THE GOSPEL TO YOU

4, 14 THE FIRST TIME. AND YOU DID NOT DESPISE OR SPIT OUT YOUR TRIAL IN MY FLESH, the temptation and testing of you that my sickness of body must have been for you. NO, YOU RECEIVED ME AS A MESSENGER

4, 15 OF GOD, AS CHRIST JESUS himself. WHERE THEN IS YOUR BLESSING for me now? FOR I will gladly TESTIFY FOR YOU THAT YOU WOULD HAVE TORN OUT YOUR

4, 16 very EYES AND GIVEN THEM TO ME. AND IS THIS THE RESULT, the end of the affair, THAT I HAVE BECOME AN ENEMY because I am TELLING YOU THE TRUTH?

4, 17 No, no, no, no, no! They are after you, THEY ARE EAGER FOR YOU but NOT IN A GOOD and healthy WAY! NO, THEY WANT TO shut you in, LOCK YOU UP, SO THAT YOU must BE dependent on them, and thus be EAGER FOR them, standing in need of

4, 18 THEM. BUT THE only GOOD state of affairs is for leaders TO BE EMULATED, sought after and followed IN WHAT IS GOOD and only in what is good—and this AT ALL TIMES—AND NOT JUST WHEN I AM PRES-

4, 19 ENT TO YOU, MY CHILDREN. Yes, I call you children, for you are my children to whom I once, with much suffering, first gave life in Christ and FOR WHOM I now AGAIN SUFFER BIRTH PANGS UNTIL CHRIST BE

4, 20 FORMED IN YOU. AND I DID SO WANT TO BE PRESENT WITH YOU NOW, AND TO CHANGE MY TONE—because I AM COMING TO MY WIT'S END WITH YOU.

4, 21 NOW YOU TELL ME, YOU WHO WANT TO BE UNDER THE LAW, DON'T YOU LISTEN TO THE LAW? Well then,

4, 22 don't you remember that IT IS WRITTEN THAT ABRA-HAM HAD TWO SONS, ONE BY A SLAVE WOMAN AND

ONE BY A FREE WOMAN? It's in the Book of Genesis. "Now Sarai, Abram's wife, bore him no children. She had an Egyptian maid whose name was Hagar; and Sarai said to Abram, 'Behold now, the Lord has prevented me from bearing children; go in to my maid; it may be that I shall obtain children by her.' And Abram hearkened to the voice of Sarai. So after Abram had dwelt ten years in the land of Canaan, Sarai, Abram's wife, took Hagar the Egyptian, her maid, and gave her to Abram her husband as a wife. And he went in to Hagar, and she conceived. . . . And Hagar bore Abram a son; and Abram called the name of his son, whom Hagar bore, Ishmael" (Genesis 16, 1–4.15).

"When Abram was ninety-nine years old the Lord appeared to Abram, and said to him, 'I am God Almighty; walk before me, and be blameless. And I will make my covenant between me and you, and will multiply you exceedingly.' Then Abram fell on his face; and God said to him, 'Behold, my covenant is with you, and you shall be the father of a multitude of nations. No longer shall your name be Abram, but your name shall be Abraham; for I have made you the father of a multitude of nations. I will make you exceedingly fruitful; and I will make nations of you, and kings shall come forth from you'. . . . And God said to Abraham, 'As for Sarai your wife, you shall not call her name Sarai, but Sarah shall be her name. I will bless her, and moreover I will give you a son by her; I will bless her, and she shall be a mother of nations; kings of peoples shall come from her'" (Genesis 17, 1–6.15–16). "And the Lord did to

121

Sarah as he had promised. And Sarah conceived, and bore Abraham a son in his old age at the time of which God had spoken to him. Abraham called the name of his son who was born to him, whom Sarah bore him, Isaac" (Genesis 21, 1–3.8–10) .

4, 23   So Abraham had these two sons. BUT THE ONE BORN OF THE SLAVE WOMAN WAS BORN ACCORDING TO THE FLESH. That is, Abraham simply did what was normal and necessary, and a child was born, according to human planning and arrangement, ends and means. BUT THE ONE FROM THE FREE WOMAN WAS BORN ACCORDING TO PROMISE. For Sarah was ninety; Abraham about a hundred. "Shall a child be born to a man who is a hundred years old? Shall Sarah, who is ninety years old, bear a child?" (Genesis 17, 17) . But Abraham believed God, did what was humanly foolish and useless, expected what was humanly impossible, and the child was born.

4, 24   Now ALL THAT IS, you know, or at least could be interpreted as AN excellent ALLEGORY of the way things are in regard to our whole question of freedom and slavery, faith and law. For HERE you can say WE HAVE TWO TESTAMENTS, two confirmed sets of dispositions of affairs by God. ONE IS the one which has to do with Abraham's heirs according to the flesh; that is FROM MOUNT SINAI, where Moses first received the Law. This covenant, one may say, is BEGETTING children FOR SLAVERY. It is the covenant which says, "Do this and you will live." It binds its followers to rules, laws, threats of punishment for specific acts performed. So that is the covenant WHICH in our allegory we will say

4, 25   IS HAGAR—MOUNT SINAI (down there IN ARABIA) —

122

the Law. She CORRESPONDS, could we not say, TO THE PRESENT DAY JERUSALEM? FOR the city of JERUSALEM, capital of Judaism today, following the covenant of Sinai, following the law of God, IS IN SERVITUDE to those laws—as we said above that everyone who would live by law is in servitude. She is in servitude, then, WITH HER CHILDREN— with all who follow or want to follow that path.

But there is another Jerusalem, a new Jerusalem,

4, 26 the heavenly city of God. This JERUSALEM, of course, the one ON HIGH, the true Jerusalem, IS FREE; and SHE IS OUR MOTHER. She is not Hagar; she is Sarah. She begets the children of promise, not children according to the flesh. She begets the children one could never humanly have expected and these children are all the nations of the earth.

4, 27 FOR IT IS WRITTEN: REJOICE, YOU BARREN ONE WHO DO NOT BEAR; BREAK OUT AND SHOUT, YOU WHO DO NOT LABOR; BECAUSE MANY ARE THE CHILDREN OF THE BARREN ONE, MORE THAN OF THE ONE WHO HAS HERSELF A HUSBAND.

4, 28 AND YOU, BROTHERS, ARE, JUST LIKE ISAAC, CHILDREN OF A PROMISE. Do you follow me? All right, what conclusion shall we draw? First of all, we won't be surprised to see the same thing happening

4, 29 once again: JUST AS AT THAT TIME THE ONE ACCORDING TO THE FLESH PERSECUTED THE ONE WHO WAS ACCORDING TO THE PROMISE, SO IS IT NOW, EXACTLY. They, the observers of the Law, are picking away at us, nagging, complaining, persecuting, because we want to live by the promise and claim the inheri-

4, 30 tance equally with them. BUT WHAT DOES THE SCRIPTURE SAY? "THROW OUT THE HANDMAID WITH

HER SON, FOR THE SON OF THE SLAVE WOMAN SHALL
4, 31   NOT INHERIT WITH THE SON OF THE FREE." AND SO
you see, the whole thing fits us and our situation,
BROTHERS: WE ARE NOT THE SONS OF A SLAVE WOMAN
BUT OF THE FREE ONE—sons of the woman, the
5, 1   heavenly Jerusalem, who is free WITH THE FREEDOM
WITH WHICH CHRIST MADE US FREE! STAND FIRM THEN.
AND DON'T GO TAKING THAT YOKE OF SLAVERY UPON
YOURSELVES AGAIN!

5, 2   LOOK, I MYSELF, PAUL, I SAY TO YOU—IF YOU GET
YOURSELF CIRCUMCISED, then you can say this:
CHRIST, the great reality of Christ, WILL BE OF NO
value, ADVANTAGE, good or importance TO YOU at
all. A terrible thought, isn't it? But I mean it. His
freedom that he won for you will not be yours to
5, 3   enjoy. AND I WITNESS AGAIN TO EVERY MAN WHO GETS
HIMSELF CIRCUMCISED, THAT HE IS OBLIGED NOW TO
5, 4   PERFORM THE WHOLE LAW OF MOSES. YOU ARE COM-
PLETELY RUINED IN REGARD TO CHRIST, YOU people WHO want to go MAKE YOURSELVES GOOD BY
observing the LAW. YOU HAVE FALLEN AWAY FROM
5, 5   GOD'S WONDERFUL FREE GIFT. FOR WE AWAIT OUR
HOPE OF JUSTICE, of personal goodness, IN SPIRIT
5, 6   AND FROM FAITH. FOR THAT IS ALL THAT COUNTS IN
CHRIST; NOT CIRCUMCISION OR NON-CIRCUMCISION BUT
FAITH, WORKING THROUGH LOVE.

5, 7   What has gone wrong? YOU WERE RUNNING WELL.
WHO HAS DECEIVED YOU and brought you TO NOT
FOLLOW THE TRUTH any longer? One thing is sure.
5, 8   This idea, THIS PERSUASION, IS NOT coming FROM
THE ONE WHO CALLED YOU! Who is responsible?
Hard to say. But it could be any one or two among
5, 9   you. "A LITTLE LEAVEN FERMENTS THE WHOLE MASS"

5, 10   as the saying goes. But now I HAVE GREAT CONFI-
DENCE IN THE LORD CONCERNING YOU THAT YOU WILL
NOT in the future THINK DIFFERENTLY about the
things that are important. AND HE WHO IS DISTURB-
ING YOU, WHOEVER HE IS, WILL BEAR THE CONDEMNA-
TION.

5, 11   AS FOR ME, BROTHERS, IF it is true I STILL PREACH
CIRCUMCISION (Have some of them been trying to
tell you that I am?) WHY AM I STILL PERSECUTED?
For if circumcision still holds, and if the Law is
still to be preached and practiced, THEN THE SCAN-
DAL OF THE CROSS IS QUITE DONE AWAY WITH. Then
there is nothing for them to get excited and angry
about. But they are plenty excited. And they're
exciting you. And now they certainly are beginning

5, 12   to anger me. God, I WISH THAT THOSE WHO ARE
GETTING YOU WORKED UP about all this circumcision
business WOULD HAVE SOMETHING OF THEIR OWN

5, 13   CHOPPED OFF [APOKOPSONTAI]. FOR YOU HAVE BEEN
CALLED to freedom and IN FREEDOM, BROTHERS.

ONLY now, one more thought, I hope it doesn't
need mentioning. YOU MUSTN'T, of course, ever LET
FREEDOM BE just A STARTING PLACE FOR giving in to
THE FLESH. You can't simply start doing anything
you feel like doing, just because there is no law to
observe. That's not the freedom of Christ. What
are you free to do? You are free THROUGH LOVE to
BECOME SLAVES TO ONE ANOTHER, to give yourselves
completely through love to perfect mutual service.
That's what freedom from law is for you: the living
out in practice of the norm of love and sacrifice
instead of obedience to prescriptions as to what to
do and how to do it. And the paradox is that this

5, 14   is the true and only fulfillment of the Law, as I think you know. FOR THE WHOLE LAW IS SUMMED UP after all IN A SINGLE WORD: YOU SHALL LOVE YOUR NEIGHBOR AS YOURSELF.

5, 15   BUT, brothers, IF YOU SNAP AT AND BITE AT ONE ANOTHER, CAREFUL THAT YOU DO NOT END instead EATING ONE ANOTHER UP!

5, 16   SO I SAY simply (instead of giving you new lists of rules to replace the old) : WALK IN THE SPIRIT. THEN YOU WON'T BE ACCOMPLISHING THE DESIRE OF

5, 17   THE FLESH. FOR FLESH HAS DESIRES THAT ARE AGAINST THE SPIRIT, AND SO does THE SPIRIT have desires that are AGAINST THE FLESH. THERE ARE THESE OPPOSED PRINCIPLES in you, you know, SO THAT IN FACT YOU DON'T ALWAYS END UP DOING WHAT YOU REALLY WANT TO DO. But that doesn't change the facts of

5, 18   the case I've been arguing. It's still true, IF YOU ARE LED BY THE SPIRIT, YOU ARE NOT UNDER LAW. I don't care how scandalous that may sound to the legalists, it is simply true. And the fact that people among you, among us, are seen to be less than paragons of perfection at every moment of their daily lives means simply that we are still human beings. But if you are led by the spirit, you

5, 19   are not under law. Now WHAT I would MEAN BY THE WORKS OF THE FLESH IS OBVIOUS enough. You all know the kind of things I mean, and you don't like them any better than I do. No one does. Things LIKE FORNICATION, UNCLEANNESS, DEBAUCH-

5, 20   ERY; again IDOLATRY, WITCHCRAFT; and ENMITIES, ANGER, ENVY, WRATHS, BITTERNESSES, SPLITS IN THE

5, 21   COMMUNITY, FACTIONS, KILLINGS, DRUNKENNESSES, CAROUSINGS, AND ALL THAT SORT OF THING. ABOUT

THESE I TELL YOU openly AS I'VE TOLD YOU BEFORE: IT'S NOT THE PEOPLE WHO DO THINGS LIKE THAT WHO ARE GOING TO INHERIT THE KINGDOM OF GOD. At least I hope not! Who would want to live in it with them?

So don't let your freedom be leading you to give the world an example of that sort of thing, crying, "Whoopee! Freedom! Now anything goes!" What kind of a follower of the cross would you be if you lived like that? No, you are in the Spirit, so let's

5, 22 see you act like men led by the spirit: THE FRUIT OF THE SPIRIT IS LOVE, JOY, PEACE; A BROAD MIND,

5, 23 GENTLENESS, GOODNESS, FAITH, MEEKNESS, SELF-RE-STRAINT. NOW AGAINST SUCH traits AS THESE and the people whose lives are marked by them, there is no law. THERE IS NO LAW!

Now that's you. Because you are of Christ. And

5, 24 THOSE WHO ARE OF CHRIST HAVE TAKEN THEIR FLESH WITH ITS PASSIONS AND DESIRES AND LEFT IT, you might say, NAILED TO THE CROSS. The cross marks their lives, the Spirit which led Christ to the cross and through it to glorious resurrection marks their

5, 25 lives—that is, your lives. So IF WE LIVE IN THE SPIRIT, as we do, having chosen our crucified Lord, then LET

5, 26 US NOW WALK IN THE SPIRIT TOO. LET US NOT START SEEKING EMPTY GLORY, PROVOKING ONE ANOTHER,

6, 1 ENVYING ONE ANOTHER. BROTHERS, EVEN IF A MAN BE CAUGHT IN SOME SIN, then YOU who are OF THE SPIRIT, spirit-filled and guided—here is what you should do: RESTORE THAT MAN, repair him, make him whole. But do it IN A SPIRIT OF GENTLENESS, WATCHING YOURSELF all the time, LEST YOU TOO BE TEMPTED.

127

For believing Christians have and accept a true responsibility for one another. Therefore they are concerned when one of their number seems to be slipping away from the high ideals their Christian life demands. They try to help such a one. You must try to help such a one. You cannot make the decision of faith for him. You cannot decide for him to bring his life into accordance with what he believes. You cannot produce the fruits of the Spirit where the Spirit itself is rendered inactive, grieved (Ephesians 4, 30) or quenched (1 Thessalonians 5, 19).

But suppose a brother who is really trying in general does commit some terrible offense against one or all of you. Suppose he violates not only "love, joy, peace, etc." (see v. 22), but even hurts, kills, robs. What to do? Well, you who notice the fault or crime, you are trying to live and walk in the Spirit, are you not? Therefore any material loss you may have suffered does not bother you so much as the fact that one of your number is dropping away and is no longer trying to walk in the spirit. So you try to help him—insofar as he wants help. You try to repair the damage he has done to his own life and that of others. But you do it not as if you were better than he. You do it with a careful and sober eye on yourself. For you know that you stand as close to a fall as he ever did. Pray and watch that you enter not into temptation.

You certainly do not in your reproof return or attempt to make him return to a norm of law. That would be to throw over everything you have been attempting. I know a simple appeal to law would be easier for you to explain, easier for him perhaps to remember and practice. To state the law, to place before his eyes the threat of the punishment any violation will receive, seems so simple, so just, and so human.

But that is not the Christian way to which I am urging you. And I want you to set that brother straight in a Christian way so that he may be again a Christian. That means you must receive him in love. You must help him to come to see the evil of a selfish action in terms of its being a falling away from the love of Christ. Murder and lying and stealing are not wrong because they are against any laws. They are wrong because they hurt—and wrong to the extent to which they do hurt—our brother for whom Christ died. Our Lord says love—and instead we hurt and abuse and exploit. That is sin for a Christian.

6, 2   BEAR ONE ANOTHER'S BURDENS, brothers; AND IN THAT WAY FULFILL THE LAW OF CHRIST. This is the only law to which you are bound. The commitments which it imposes on you will vary from one individual instance to another, however. They cannot be defined in advance. Your law is love—and in the concrete it is: bear the other person's burden, whatever that may turn out to be. Is he in pain, sorrow, suffering? Is he hungry, thirsty, homeless? Is he caught in sin? Wavering in faith? Afraid of life? Has he no job? Does he stand in need of schooling? No matter what the problem of the other person is, it becomes your problem. That is the law with which Christ sends us out to live our Christian lives.

Do you foresee that if you took that seriously, you could not really be of help to more than one or two others? Try it anyway. For there is a magic in the method: the magic of self-multiplication, the wonder of growth. For one person who seriously lives this way today, there will be two tomorrow —and perhaps a hundred one week later. Christian reform through personal love does not draw up a blueprint for the salvation of the world, a blueprint which you alone carry the responsibility of bringing to actual completion. It does not propound a system. It does not sketch or create an organization. Men in their sincere desire to love and do good to as many of their fellow men as possible may well take such devices as these. Their good intentions deserve blessing, and their partial successes merit our rejoicing. But the gospel way proposes something far simpler. Whether it is more efficacious or not, cannot be answered apart from decision to believe or not to believe. For the gospel way proposes simply doing what you can in a personal, human way. Loving intensely and completely those whom life brings within your reach, and doing for them all the good you can. Loving them unto death—your death. The grand overall planning and program in the Christian "system" is left to the Lord himself, who has promised us our efforts in faith will indeed succeed.

So "bear one another's burdens" is our law, the law of Christ. This means love. This means self-sacrifice. For each of us has enough burdens of his own. But the gospel calls him to take on himself the burdens of others as well. For Christ did this for us, taking on himself the burden of our sins and dying for us on the cross.

This is the only excellence we have—attempted adhesion to the law he proclaimed in dying for us.

6, 3 Fulfill that law, no other. FOR IF ANYONE THINKS THAT HE IS SOMETHING, WHEREAS IN REALITY HE IS NOTHING, HE DECEIVES HIMSELF. But that is exactly the situation of anyone who attempts a morality of law, and thinks that his own achievements and fulfillments and lists of good deeds are impressively to his credit before God. Before God we are nothing. Let us then learn to think of ourselves as nothing. Let us not look to a series of commandments which we can pride ourselves on fulfilling one by one. Let us look to Christ crucified and the law of perfect love his cross proclaims; and let us be ashamed at our failures, our weakness, our sloth when we compare ourselves with that action of his.

6, 4 AND LET EACH ONE TEST HIS OWN WORK AND THEN if he is to take any pride or glory at all, HE WILL HAVE HIS GLORY in comparing himself ONLY TO HIMSELF AND NOT TO ANY OTHER MAN. FOR before God's

6, 5 judgment seat EACH ONE WILL CARRY HIS OWN LOAD.

6, 6 Another thing, LET HIM WHO IS BEING TAUGHT THE WORD SHARE IN ALL GOOD THINGS WITH THE ONE WHO IS TEACHING HIM. That is only right and good, and a true Christian way of showing appreciation and love. That way certain members of the community who are found most fit for such a task may be able to give all or most of their time to the work of studying the word and instructing others in the word. Whereas if they had to continue according to my own example (Paul always worked with his hands for his own support), they would not have much time left over from their regular daily work to minister to the Lord's people directly.

Now get this right and straight from the beginning! I am not imposing an obligation on any Christian. I am only pointing out what you will probably want to be doing of your own free will. For the community will suffer if there are not enough people free enough to devote themselves to a study of God's word and to the attempt to explain it to new converts, to preach and exhort the faithful community with it. You need men free enough and willing enough to do these things. And that means their support must come from someplace.

But what you do not need is another priestly class to replace the priestly and hierarchical class of the Old Covenant from which you have so recently escaped. Trained specialists you do need. But better let them be mere part-time servants than have them become a class of drones, living off the rest of you without need or justification.

But in a thriving, healthy community this will be no problem. Some men will devote themselves to the ministry and the rest of you will rejoice to make it possible for them to continue to do so, just as you often tried to offer gifts freely to me (see Philippians 4, 14f.). If the day ever arrives when a man or group, commissioned by you to preach the gospel, ceases to do so or ceases to be diligent in the way he does it, then of course he is not the "one who teaches the word," and you are not in his regard "the ones who are being instructed in the word." And therefore you will stop sharing with him your material goods, just as he has ceased to share truly spiritual goods with you.

6, 7   DO NOT BE DECEIVED; GOD IS NOT MOCKED. FOR WHATEVER A MAN SOWS THAT IS WHAT HE WILL REAP

6, 8   TOO. BECAUSE HE WHO SOWS INTO HIS OWN FLESH WILL REAP CORRUPTION FROM THE FLESH; AND HE WHO SOWS INTO THE SPIRIT WILL REAP FROM THE

6, 9   SPIRIT ETERNAL LIFE. AND LET US NOT GROW WEARY IN DOING GOOD, FOR WE WILL REAP truly AT THE

6, 10   PROPER TIME, IF WE DO NOT LOSE COURAGE. ALL RIGHT THEN, WHILE WE HAVE TIME, LET US WORK WHAT IS GOOD IN REGARD TO ALL MEN, AND ESPECIALLY IN REGARD TO OUR FELLOWS IN THE ONE HOUSE OF THE FAITH.

6, 11   SEE WITH WHAT LARGE LETTERS I HAVE WRITTEN TO YOU WITH MY OWN HAND!

6, 12   AS MANY AS WANT TO MAKE A GOOD SHOWING IN FLESH, THESE ARE THE ONES WHO ARE COMPELLING YOU TO BE CIRCUMCISED. They do it ONLY SO AS NOT TO BE PERSECUTED FOR THE CROSS OF CHRIST. They are afraid of the persecutions which loom over us Christians—first from those Jews who have not believed in Jesus as Christ, and especially from their leaders who put our Lord to death. But they also fear persecution from the Romans—for if we do not follow the Jewish law, we cannot claim exemption any longer with certitude under the special Roman provisions for the Jews.

Am I terribly unjust in saying that this fear is their real motive, and not simply sincere zeal for

6, 13   the Law? I think so, FOR NOT EVEN THE CIRCUMCISED THEMSELVES DO KEEP THE LAW. BUT THEY WANT YOU TO BE CIRCUMCISED. Why? IN ORDER THAT THEY MAY GLORY IN YOUR FLESH. That's at least part of their motivation.

6, 14   And myself? I want no glory but one: MAY IT NEVER HAPPEN TO ME TO BE ABLE TO GLORY IN ANYTHING BUT THE CROSS OF OUR LORD JESUS CHRIST. THROUGH HIM THE WORLD IS CRUCIFIED TO ME AND I

6, 15   TO THE WORLD. FOR CIRCUMCISION IS NOTHING AND NEITHER IS A FORESKIN. BUT A NEW CREATION IS

6, 16   EVERYTHING. AND AS MANY AS WILL WALK IN THIS RULE—PEACE AND MERCY BE ON THEM—AND ON GOD'S ISRAEL.

6, 17   FOR THE REST, LET NO ONE PROVIDE ME TROUBLES —FOR I BEAR THE MARKS OF JESUS IN MY BODY.

6, 18   THE GRACE OF OUR LORD JESUS CHRIST BE WITH YOUR SPIRIT, BROTHERS. AMEN.